♥ Build Your Own ♥

ROMANTIC COMEDY

• Build Your Own •

ROMANTIC COMEDY

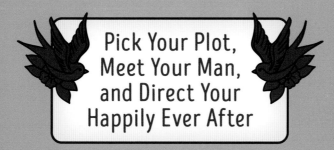

Pick Your Plot,
Meet Your Man,
and Direct Your
Happily Ever After

♥ Lana Schwartz ♥

ULYSSES PRESS

Published in the United States by:
Ulysses Press
P. O. Box 3440
Berkeley, CA 94703
www.ulyssespress.com

ISBN: 978-1-64604-005-6
Library of Congress Control Number: 2019951367

Printed in the United States by Versa Press
10 9 8 7 6 5 4 3 2 1

Acquisitions editor: Bridget Thoreson
Managing editor: Claire Chun
Editor: Lauren Harrison
Proofreader: Renee Rutledge
Front cover and interior design: Malea Clark-Nicholson
Layout: what!design @ whatweb.com
Artwork: shutterstock.com and graphicpear.com

For my mom and dad

Contents

PICK YOUR PLOT

Which rom com path is the one for you? Take the quiz here to find out or turn to Chapter One and pick any of the options there!

WHAT DO YOU LOOK FOR IN A GUY?

A. Someone who reminds me of my past.
B. Royal blood.
C. Someone who challenges me.
D. A guy I can meet at work.
E. A man who sees my full potential.
F. Someone who wants to bankrupt my company.
G. Power.

PICK A PROFESSION.

A. Record store owner.
B. Queen of a small, lesser-known country.
C. Data entry.
D. Editor-in-chief of a female-focused magazine.
E. I prefer not to talk about money.
F. Bookseller/barista/baker.
G. Journalist.

WHAT'S YOUR FAVORITE DRINK?

A. Moscow Mule.
B. Red wine.
C. Anything strong works fine.
D. Tequila.
E. Champagne, preferably opened on the deck of a yacht.
F. Coffee.
G. Whiskey, neat.

WHAT'S YOUR FAVORITE CITY?

A. I prefer small towns.
B. Prague.
C. Anywhere would be better than here.
D. San Francisco, Chicago, somewhere like that.
E. Newport, Rhode Island.
F. New York City, is there anywhere else?
G. Any city free from corruption.

Mostly As:

Back to your hometown you go to reconnect with your high school crush. Turn to the rose on page 4.

Mostly Bs:

We see a prince in your future. Begin at the rose on page 4.

Mostly Cs:

You're not thrilled with your dead-end job, but that doesn't mean there's not something better in your future. Start at the palm tree on page 5.

Mostly Ds:

You've got a magazine to save! Turn to the sun on page 2.

Mostly Es:

Has anyone ever mistaken you for someone else, or told you that you remind them of someone? Start off at the palm tree on page 5 to get a taste of what *their* life might be like.

Mostly Fs:

You're all about that bookstore life. Turn to the coffee cup on page 6.

Mostly Gs:

Something's up at the mayor's office, and you're determined to find out what it is. Turn to the pencil on page 8.

CAST OF CHARACTERS

JENNY: Our plucky heroine who gets back up every time she gets knocked down, again and again—and well, again. She believes women can have it all—both a great relationship and a killer career— and she's not going to stop until she has the best of both. Anne Hathaway in *The Devil Wears Prada*, with hints of Meg Ryan in all of the Nora Ephron movies and a twist of Kate Hudson in *How to Lose a Guy in 10 Days*.

TOM: That guy who drives you absolutely crazy, but you just can't stay away from. Smart, funny, handsome, and he knows it. A suave and smooth talker who might make you roll your eyes, but you'd still rather listen to him talk than anyone else. James Marsden in *27 Dresses* and Glen Powell in *Set It Up*, mixed with Henry Golding from *Crazy Rich Asians* and Mark Ruffalo in *13 Going on 30*.

DAVE: A scruffy, lovable guy, who just wants a nice girl to watch his favorite TV show with. Isn't that really what life is all about, anyway? Think Bill Pullman in *Sleepless in Seattle* meets Chris Pratt in *Bride Wars*.

CJ: Jenny's BFF, who's always there to lend an ear, or a wisecrack when Jenny needs it most, but that doesn't mean she doesn't have her own needs, wants, or desires. Judy Greer in basically every romantic comedy she's ever been in.

NATASHA: Your classic rom com villain, who has the man you want, or is actively plotting to steal him from you. Impossibly gorgeous, sophisticated, and seemingly everything you're not. Cameron Diaz in *My Best Friend's Wedding*, if she were a bad person, or Tess from *27 Dresses*.

CYNTHIA: That impossible-to-please rom com boss, who seems to exist only to make your life miserable, but every once in a while, if you look closely, an ounce of vulnerability seems to shine through. Meryl Streep in *The Devil Wears Prada*, obviously, plus Lucy Liu in *Set It Up*.

CECILIA: A ritzy, proper type who hasn't stepped below 59th Street in Manhattan in at least 30 years, if ever. Think Susan Sullivan in *My Best Friend's Wedding*, or Candice Bergen in *Bride Wars*.

MAURICIO: The man who's here to make you an entirely new woman. Your fairy godfather, if you will. Larry Miller in *The Princess Diaries*, or Hector Elizondo in *Pretty Woman*.

THE QUEEN: Regal and impossibly intimidating, the Queen knows what's best for everyone, even if they can't see it for themselves. Julie Andrews in *The Princess Diaries* meets Michelle Yeoh in *Crazy Rich Asians*.

Chapter One

INTRODUCTIONS

It's a beautiful day in New York City. The sun is shining. The chirping birds are as loud as the tiny children who populate this West Village neighborhood are quiet. Jenny doesn't wait for the "Walk" sign as she crosses the street— the "Walk" sign waits for her. It's the kind of morning that makes her remember why she moved here from her small town in another, less important part of America. The kind of morning that makes it seems like her dreams are within reach. Because they are! If things go well at work today—which they will, because they have to—she'll be even closer to showing the world that she is *somebody*.

She arrives at her favorite coffee shop at 9:10 a.m., 10 minutes later than she normally does, which means she's 10 minutes behind schedule, and *that* means Jenny can only spend two minutes at the coffee shop, rather than her usual allotted five minutes. Because if she spends her usual five minutes at the coffee shop, she'll be late for work—and she *cannot* be late for work. Not today.

> *It's the kind of morning that makes her remember why she moved here from her small town in another, less important part of America. The kind of morning that makes it seems like her dreams are within reach.*

Jenny picks up her scalding-hot, triple-shot, extra-large latte and heads toward the door, ready to take on the day.

But then, out of nowhere—*thud*—and the latte has been spilled all over her meticulously chosen, *very* expensive, dry-clean-only white blouse.

"Oh my god, oh my god, oh my god. This can't be happening," she says.

"Napkin?" asks the source of the thud. A man. Of course. He holds a napkin out to her, but the expression on his face is too smug to render it a peace offering.

"You're not going to apologize for knocking into me?" Jenny asks, grabbing the napkin stubbornly. She does need one, after all.

"Why would I apologize? You knocked into me," the man replies. And OK, if someone held a gun to Jenny's head and asked, "Is this man the best-looking man you've ever seen in your life?" she would say yes, but failing that, she will never, ever, ever admit out loud that he is attractive.

"You *clearly* knocked into me," Jenny replies. Her blood boils, or something like that.

"Then why are you the one covered in coffee?" the man says, flashing her a knowing smile.

 To follow Jenny to the magazine where she works, turn to the magazine on page 15.

 If Jenny can't worry about this mysterious stranger right now because she has a big date with her boyfriend tonight, turn to the rose on page 4.

It's one of those perfect evenings. The kind that makes Jenny feel like maybe magic really is possible after all. There's a gentle breeze in the summer air, and you can see between three and five stars in the sky—the most possible in Jenny's major metropolitan city. She's having dinner with her boyfriend. She's, without a doubt, absolutely certain that tonight is the night that he is going to finally, *finally* propose. She spent hours picking out her outfit with her best friend, CJ (It's a pale pink shift dress with an empire waist that screams bridal.) She even did ring finger exercises to ensure her finger was strong enough to withstand the weight of even the biggest rock. She promised her parents she'd call them as soon as dinner's over. And said boyfriend has taken her to one of the fanciest restaurants in the entire city. They've got the best table in the house, right next to the window, with a view overlooking the city. The restaurant bustles with customers, all of whom, Jenny is sure, are looking at their table and wondering, "Who is this handsome couple? Surely they must be important people to snag that prime real estate." The city lights and the candlelight on the table both reflect into Jenny's boyfriend's eyes, which bore into her deeply.

"We've been together a long, long time," he begins. "I've been doing a lot of thinking." *This* is the moment. And in this moment, he:

 Proposes! Yes! Turn to the ring on page 25.

 Ugh, doesn't propose. Turn to the broken heart on page 26.

"Another margarita?" Jenny hears a voice asking, as she lazily reclines on a tropical beach somewhere, wearing a chic neon yellow one-piece bathing suit, a gigantic black straw hat, and Jackie O. sunglasses that cover most of her face.

She looks up to find that the voice is coming from a tan, handsome man. She nods and smiles. He hands her the margarita.

"You know, I have something I need to get off my chest," he tells Jenny.

"You can tell me anything," she replies. This is gonna be good.

"I think it's time..." he says, slowly, "...that you get up and go to work."

Suddenly, Jenny hears a series of incredibly loud beeps, and with a slam of the snooze button, she is firmly off Romantic Dream Island and back in the realm of her bedroom. Where she sleeps. Alone.

"Another dream ruined by waking up," Jenny says out loud to no one. She moseys around her tiny, gray studio apartment, the size of which is more appropriate for a litter of small children than a grown woman. It remains largely undecorated, scattered with moving boxes, even though she's lived there for years now.

She keeps doing that thing where she buys posters and has every intention of getting them framed and hanging them, but she never does. She tells her friends that she will, but she is lying.

Even though it's not yet light outside, Jenny bundles up in her winter clothes and drives to work at her meaningless, unfulfilling, soul-crushing job at Data Solutions, Inc.

 To follow Jenny and her tan, handsome man, turn to the puppy on page 18.

 Do you want to see Jenny embark on an adventure that turns her life upside down? Turn to the lotus on page 22.

"The charming Toffee and Coffee never ceases to delight and is the number one destination for any toffee and coffee lover who finds themselves in the tri-state area." — *The New York Observer*, 1995

"Thirty years after its opening, the cozy haven for Manhattan sweet tooths Toffee and Coffee is expanding into Toffee, Coffee, and Co. The always-packed candy shop is expanding into treats of all sorts, and will acquire the bookshop next door, West Side Books, allowing the bookstore's current owners to retire early to Florida." — *The Village Voice*, 2010

"As hyper-gentrification increasingly continues to shake the neighborhood, leaving local business after local business empty in its wake, one has to wonder how much longer the ones left standing—like the nostalgic Toffee, Coffee, and Co.—will be, well, left standing." — *Grub Street*, 2019

"Will you stop looking at that already?" CJ, Jenny's BFF and employee, asks her. Jenny quickly slams her laptop shut. CJ has curly brown hair, which serves as a nice contrast to Jenny's straight hair—which can only be appropriately described as "honey-colored"—that she sometimes runs a curling iron through for a nice beachy wave effect.

"I'm not looking at anything! I'm ordering...caramel from our vendor," Jenny replies, lying.

"These sites are constantly predicting the apocalypse of small businesses, and here we are, standing strong after 100 years," CJ says.

"Do you tell customers that we've been open for 100 years? Because we've been open for 30 years. You've worked here for three of them."

"Well then I look forward to celebrating Toffee, Coffee, and Co.'s centennial," CJ concludes.

"In....," CJ goes silent for a moment, clearly counting in her head, but coming up short on an answer. Jenny waits a beat for CJ to volunteer the answer on her own, but she never does. Classic CJ.

"Seventy years," Jenny tells CJ, helping her out.

"Seventy years! I knew that."

They high five and smile. But their joy is short-lived.

If a handsome man who will change everything comes into Toffee, Coffee, and Co., turn to the candy on page 11.

 Enough with the coffee shop/bookstore/bakery, Jenny has a big date with her boyfriend tonight! Turn to the rose on page 4.

"Staff meeting! Staff meeting, now!" A loud, booming voice rings out across the newsroom.

"Do you have anything?" Jenny asks her cubicle mate and best friend, CJ, peeking over the divider that separates their desks.

"No—do you?" CJ squeals, panicked.

"Oh God, no," Jenny replies.

"The star reporter of the *Sun Gazette Tribune* doesn't have three different leads she's working simultaneously? Tsk, tsk. I never thought I'd see the day," CJ says, reprimanding her. Jenny takes it in stride, though, because after all, she really is the star reporter and usually she is working three different leads simultaneously. They make their way from the cubicles across the drab, off-white newsroom and enter the also drab, off-white conference room where the rest of the newspaper's reporters sit at a round table, anxiously poring over pages of longhand notes on their steno pads.

> Jenny takes it in stride, though, because after all, she really is the star reporter and usually she is working three different leads simultaneously.

"Pitch me! I want to hear pitches," Jenny's extremely formidable boss, Cynthia, says in that same booming voice, charging into the room like it's a boxing ring and slamming the door behind them. She has a pixie cut and wears slacks, and everyone is terrified of her.

One writer begins timidly: "There's a new park that's opening for children—"

"A new park? For children? How precious," Cynthia says in a mimicking baby voice, resting her palms on the table and staring the writer—who now is wondering if they will have to pack up their desk today, and if so, how long will that take—straight in the face.

"This, lest you have forgotten, is the *Sun Gazette Tribune*. We speak truth to power and expose corruption. You want to write about park openings? Go to the *Daily Globe*."

The writer now appears to be on the verge of tears. Jenny knows that if someone doesn't speak up with a good idea soon, Cynthia will continue her diatribe about

power and corruption and her gonzo journalism days with Hunter S. Thompson in the 1970s until everyone is crying, asleep, or somehow both.

"Mayor! The new mayor," Jenny pipes up, her thoughts not yet fully fleshed out, but so desperate to avoid listening to her boss fondly recall her San Francisco acid trips that she'd report on anything.

"I'm listening," Cynthia replies, now staring Jenny down, somewhat approvingly—although she doesn't want *her* to know that.

"I saw that the new mayor is looking for an assistant. I'll go undercover and we can expose the real agenda he has for the city," Jenny explains, now twirling a gnawed-on No. 2 pencil between her fingers. "I mean, his parents own half the city—there's no way he has the interests of the common people at heart." The corners of Cynthia's mouth turn up ever so slightly and Jenny can tell—she stuck the landing.

 Want to see Jenny with a very sweet—but boring—boyfriend? Turn to the take-out box on page 27.

 Ready for heartbreak? If Jenny gets dumped, turn to the broken heart on page 26.

Chapter Two

MEET CUTES

"Hello?" A deep voice calls out from the front of the store, in an accent that's distinctly European, although not British.

"Coming!" Jenny replies, throwing on her Toffee, Coffee, and Co. apron and carrying out a tray of still-hot toffee.

And that's when she sees him. A Disney cartoon prince come to life. In her store.

And, of course, right when he turns around, that's exactly when Jenny drops the tray of hot toffee on the floor, spilling it everywhere.

"Let me help you with that," he says, again in that confusing, hard-to-place accent.

"Oh, don't be silly," Jenny replies, feeling dizzy. She definitely ate this morning, right? Why can't she remember if she had anything to eat today? Why can't she remember anything from her life before this very moment?

Jenny bends down to pick it up, and of course, so does he.

They bump heads.

He and Jenny both recoil in pain, but then, at that moment, their eyes find each other. Jenny is absolutely certain, beyond a shadow of a doubt, that this man is her soulmate. Her other half. The missing puzzle piece. Someone she can wear matching flannel shirts with when they pose for their annual holiday cards they send to their friends and family.

They stay like that, locking eyes, with still-hot toffee on the ground between them for what feels like an eternity. But before Jenny can continue to contemplate the nature of time, she hears CJ call from the back room.

"Hey, do you think I could get out of here early tonight? I have a date with—" CJ says, before she sees Jenny in the middle of a swoon-worthy session with some model out of a J. Crew catalog.

"Yeah, go for it," Jenny says, still coming down from her ethereal encounter. She picks up the tray of toffee, embarrassed.

"Can I get you anything?" Jenny asks him.

"Yes, um, I'll take 15 boxes of your best toffee, this copy of *White Teeth* by Zadie Smith, a cup of tea...and your phone number."

Flummoxed, Jenny replies, "Anything for you." She blushes. He smiles. She quickly corrects herself. "I mean, coming right up. "

Jenny rings him up for $500 and gives him her business card.

 Is Toffee, Coffee, and Co. in trouble? If so, turn to the cupcake on page 17.

 Want to learn more about this mysterious stranger's family life? Turn to the sofa on page 24.

Lost. Jenny is lost. In the 21st century, when everyone has an internet-powered map in their pocket, she still manages to get lost. It's embarrassing, really.

The thing is, these streets are windy. And they have cute, folksy names—no grid system here. Plus, not all of the storefronts are numbered, which makes it very hard to know which direction you're going.

"I guess I'll just have to do this the old-fashioned way," Jenny says to herself.

She grits her teeth and taps a man nearby on the back of the shoulder.

"Excuse me, do you know where—" Jenny begins, and then abruptly stops.

"Where your Bikini Kill CD is? I told you I gave it back to you after I borrowed it." It was Tom. After all of these years—Tom. What a wonderfully common name. Her best friend from the age of 5 until 15. She hasn't seen him since they graduated high school.

"How have you been? It's been, like, a million years," Jenny says, suddenly forgetting the fact that she's lost and that she has somewhere she needs to be in the first place. "You look so... different." By different, obviously, she means hot, and he knows it.

"Hah, well, a late-in-life growth spurt and a prescription for Proactiv can go a long way," Tom retorts.

"What are you doing now?" Jenny inquires, hoping his answer will be a simple, *nothing at all.* "Want to get a drink? Or five, perhaps?"

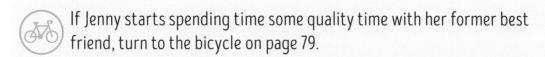

If Jenny starts spending time some quality time with her former best friend, turn to the bicycle on page 79.

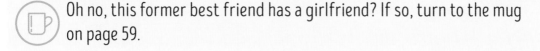

Oh no, this former best friend has a girlfriend? If so, turn to the mug on page 59.

Chapter Three

INCITING INCIDENTS

Finally, Jenny arrives at her job at *Woman Magazine*, in the tallest skyscraper smack dab in the middle of Manhattan, her formerly pristine white shirt covered in cold coffee. When she reaches her office on the 88th floor, her BFF, CJ, is there waiting. She holds a replacement blouse in one hand and a fresh cup of coffee in the other.

"Wow, have some shirt with your coffee?" CJ asks. CJ always had a knack for lightening the mood, even when certain moods should not be lightened.

Jenny and CJ walk from the elevator to her desk—their four-inch heels clacking underneath them—discussing the cool, new bar they plan to go to that night. It's a speakeasy that *also* has board games.

Before Jenny can swap out the coffee-stained top for the new one CJ brought her, she sees that horrible man (with great teeth) from the coffee shop who ruined her shirt getting off the elevator.

What is he doing here? First *her* coffee shop and now *her* office? What else could go wrong today?

And just then, she sees her boss, Cynthia—who hates everyone except her ancient Persian cat, Miuccia, and her therapist—walk over to that very same horrible man (with twinkling eyes) and shake his hand like they're...friends...or something? Or like she is capable of feeling affection for another human being. This is stunning.

"Minions. I have an announcement to make," Cynthia announces in her affected way of speaking that's not an accent so much as a dialect that belongs solely to people who own their own islands.

"It's like she came out of the womb saying 'Bad. No. Wrong. Get me a vodka tonic, hold the tonic!'" CJ whispers to Jenny. Jenny cackles.

Cynthia walks to the front of the office, welcoming the horrible man (who happens to have a jawline sharper than Wisconsin cheddar), perhaps even...smiling at him like he's a rare sub-Saharan blood diamond or the original *Breakfast at Tiffany's* Givenchy dress.

"Everyone. Look at me. This is Tom," Cynthia announces to the office. "He's here to help *Woman* magazine appeal to men. OK. Now stop looking at me. You! Don't look at me."

"Jenny!" she barks.

"Yes, Ma'am."

"Do not call me 'ma'am.' 'Ma'am' is a gendered term used to describe old women and *I* am not old. Would an old woman know what ethical nonmonogamy is and use CBD oil without prejudice?"

"No...I guess not."

"Exactly. And because you, Jenny, are the best writer at *Woman*, I am entrusting you with taking Tom under your wing."

Before she or Tom can protest, Cynthia says, "I don't recommend protesting, as I have already made up my mind and historically no one has ever changed it before, except the one time at Studio 54 when Elton John told me I should get fringe. That's what British people call bangs. I expect a fully fleshed-out new plan for the magazine by next week. I'll be in my office, just, *you know*, running the magazine." No one knows exactly what Cynthia does, but only she can do it.

This guy, who yes, maybe is good-looking but will *never* win Jenny over, smiles at her. Again she feels like her blood is boiling, or something like that.

"More coffee?" he asks.

 If Jenny and Tom have to work on a presentation together, turn to the easel on page 46.

 If Jenny and Tom need to go on a road trip together (for work-related reasons, obviously), turn to the car on page 49.

 Does Jenny decide to embrace her outdoorsy side with Tom? Turn to the mountains on page 44.

 If Jenny takes her glasses off (gasp), turn to the pizza on page 71.

"We're doomed! Doomed," Dave announces, walking into the store, wearing a messenger bag with patches on it. Dave is alternative. "Doomed."

"What are you talking about?" asks Jenny, as she and CJ ice a fresh batch of cupcakes. "And you're 15 minutes late for work."

Dave holds up an important-looking envelope.

"What's this?" Jenny asks, grabbing it from him.

"It's a letter from the landlord. Like half the block has gotten one."

"Mrs. Haggersham? She's a sweet old lady. It's probably an ordinance or zoning thing. Calm down. And get to work." Jenny throws him an apron from behind the counter, opens the envelope, and begins to read aloud.

"As you know, it has been the honor of my life to preside over the premises of Toffee, Coffee, and Co. for the last five decades," Jenny says. "See? It's been her honor," Jenny asserts, confidently. She continues reading.

"But the time has come for me to pass the baton." Before Jenny can finish, CJ squeezes the icing tube in her hand. Hard. Icing flies everywhere.

But Jenny continues reading, now crestfallen. "I have sold my properties to Thor Equity Capital Liquidators, Inc. They will be your new landlord. Effective immediately. Forever yours, Mrs. Haggersham."

"What does this mean?" CJ asks, concerned.

"I think it means the end of Toffee, Coffee, and Co.," Jenny replies, holding back tears. CJ nods solemnly before dabbing a chunk of icing out of Jenny's hair with her finger and sucking on it.

 If it's the Tom who, as it turns out, owns half of Manhattan, who's the reason why the bookstore is going out of business, turn to the book on page 68.

 If Jenny can't think about the store right now because she has a big date with Tom tonight, turn to the ring on page 27.

For all intents and purposes, Jenny has a very, very important report that she is working on. That being said, in the last hour, she's typed exactly...three words.

As much as she'd like to concentrate on the task in front of her, she simply cannot, not with the object of her five-year-long affection working in such close proximity, at least: Dave—her friend, her coworker—who has no idea she's alive, while she spends her days watching him run his fingers through his long hair. Or laughing along quietly at the YouTube videos she emails him of puppies dancing like humans. OK, OK, he obviously knows she's alive, she'll concede that much, but he doesn't *notice* her. Not the way she wants him to, at least. Her best friend CJ is always telling her to "go for it!" Jenny didn't even know in which way to "go" that would bring her closer to "it."

"Jenny! Hey, Jenny!" Ugh. Tom. Jenny ignores him. She's not in the mood to deal with this. He balls up a piece of paper and throws it at her face.

"What?" she asks him, and he grins widely. Fine. Now he has her attention.

"Did you finish that report?" Wow, an extremely annoying question from her extremely annoying coworker. Jenny can't say she's surprised.

"It's...coming along," she says, lying.

"Well, let me know if you need any help," he tells her, incredibly rudely, in Jenny's opinion.

And just when Jenny is about to really dig into her report (for real this time, she *swears*), Dave stands up and takes his cardigan off to reveal the blue button-down shirt he's wearing underneath, throwing Jenny completely off-track once again.

Noticing the blank expression on Jenny's face and the source of her distraction, Tom waves his hands in front of her eyeline.

"What do you see in that guy?" Tom asks, mystified that every woman in the office seemingly has the hots for that twerp.

"For starters, he's smart, worldly, attractive, good at his job, nice, polite..." Jenny continues in this vein until Tom finally cuts her off.

"Boring, cookie cutter, an alien from planet Dull."

"It doesn't matter anyway. He doesn't see me like that," Jenny says, dejectedly.

"Well, that's not about you. It's all perception. Change the way he sees you."

At this, Jenny scoffs. "Oh, like it's so easy."

"It absolutely is. I bet you that I can get Dave to ask you on a date."

Jenny considers this. "And what do you get if you win?"

"Other than bragging rights? You write my reports for six months."

"And if I'm right, and there's no possible way to get Dave to be interested in me? You'll write my reports for six months?" Tom nods.

Jenny weighs the possibilities in her head. What's the worst that could happen?

> Another wonderful thing about Dave—he always sees the best in people, so he can never tell when someone is making fun of him.

"Deal," she tells him, and they shake on it.

"Hey! What are you guys talking about over there?" Dave asks, calling out from his desk.

Jenny immediately turns beet red. Tom, ever the jokester, replies, "We're talking about you, bud." Tom sends a smirk Dave's way and Dave, who has no choice but to assume Tom is joking, laughs unsurely for a second before returning to his work. Jenny sighs. Another wonderful thing about Dave—he always sees the best in people, so he can never tell when someone is making fun of him.

Tom looks back at Jenny and winks. "This is gonna be fun."

 If Jenny and Tom start spending more time together, turn to the bicycle on page 79.

 If Jenny decides to embrace her outdoorsy side, turn to the mountains on page 44.

Jenny is at the end of her rope. She doesn't know where she was going, but she knows she can't be *here* anymore. She has to put at least 10,000 miles between herself and this godforsaken city and everyone in it.

But where to go? Somewhere idyllic, obviously. And charming. A small town, where everyone knows each other's names.

"Idyllic," "charming," and "small town where everyone knows each other's names" are the exact search terms Jenny enters into Google as she guzzles down a glass of red wine and chomps on a slice of pepperoni pizza. She's sitting on her bed wearing her favorite pair of black leggings and her Kale Without Fail sweatshirt, her favorite outfit for pizza-eating. She begins to envision a place where people will be wowed by her big-city smarts; her city-slicker attitude; basically, the fact that she...lived in a city. A place where she can meet a man who knows how to catch a fish with his bare hands, but also knows to release it because many species of sea life are radically overfished.

Immediately, a hit: "This Charming Town Is the Perfect Place to Go When You Need to Get Away from It All," the article promises.

Smalton, USA.

Fuck.

"Smalton, USA, is a charming river town that represents the best of what America has to offer. A place where you can get a damn good cup of coffee and actually enjoy it with the people around you. It's a place anyone would be lucky to call their hometown," the article reads in part.

Sounds perfect...minus the fact that Smalton happens to be Jenny's actual hometown, a place she hasn't been in at least 10 years. And a place she didn't feel so lucky to call her hometown when she actually lived there.

Is it time to go back home again?

> Smalton, USA, is a charming river town that represents the best of what America has to offer. A place where you can get a damn good cup of coffee and actually enjoy it with the people around you.

If you want Jenny to go back home and subsequently reunite with her childhood crush, turn to the compass on page 13.

 If you want Jenny to stick it out at *Woman Magazine*, turn to the easel on page 46.

"Another day, another zero dollars," Jenny says to herself, lighting up a cigarette as she stands on the street during her 15-minute break.

"Hello! Hello!" Suddenly, Jenny sees a ritzy-looking woman in an impeccably tailored lemon meringue puff of a skirt suit, waving at her manically.

Jenny blows out her last plume of smoke and crushes her cigarette below her boot.

"Is this where you've been hiding out? No one has seen you since you left for the ashram!"

"Ashram?" Jenny replies, confused. She won't even download the Headspace app. Who does this one-percenter think she is?

"Yes, the ashram! You left for the ashram five years ago and no one has seen you since!"

Jenny continues to stare at the woman, unabashedly puzzled, which, in turn, puzzles the ritzy woman. But suddenly, the ritzy woman has a revelation, one that clears up her clouds of confusion.

"You must have forgotten all of us while you were away for so long, silently meditating. I'm your mom's best friend, *Cecilia*," she says, sounding out each syllable, "*and* the executor of her and your father's will. I know when you ran away to that ashram you said you didn't want their life for yourself, but the inheritance, the Upper East Side classic six, the Newport estate, the Paris pied-à-terre, *and* the yacht are all in your name, whenever you want them."

Inheritance? Now Jenny is listening.

"I suffered a partial memory loss!" Jenny bursts out, shouting a little too loudly. "While I was at the ashram. I hit my head really hard one day and I don't remember a thing about my life before I left."

Will this woman believe her? Jenny wonders. Are rich people really that naïve? Cecilia pulls her into a tight hug. "You poor, poor dear. Come with me and we'll get you sorted out." OK, Jen thinks, at least this rich person is that naïve.

"And to be clear, you do spell your name J-e-n-n-i-e, correct? And not J-e-n-n-y?" Cecilia asks, pulling away slightly. "That is the only thing that would stop me from thinking you're not who you say you are."

"...Yes," Jenny says, quickly lying. Cecilia hugs her again. This was going to be fun.

 If Jenny says, "Screw it, why not?" and heads to Newport with Cecilia, turn to the pillar on page 51.

 If Jenny decides she's not actually up for this con and heads back inside to work, turn to the puppy on page 18.

"Listen, I have something I need to tell you," Tom tells Jenny, sitting her down on his green leather couch, located left and center in his sprawling bachelor pad. "Something I should've told you as soon as we met." He stares at her deeply, intensely, his green eyes—that just so happen to be the very same shade of green as his couch—shining.

"Ah, the thing every girl dreams of hearing," Jenny says, attempting to break the tension. But it doesn't work. Tom continues to stare at her intently.

"I don't know how to say this, but...I'm...a prince," Tom tells Jenny.

"A Prince...fan? Who isn't?" Jenny replies, confused.

"No. I mean, yes, I do like Prince. But I am the crown prince of Snelgravia."

"Snelgravia?"

"Yes, it's sandwiched between Genovia and Aldovia, southeast of the Baltic Sea." Tom picks up the globe from its place on his fine chocolate-brown end table. He spins it until it lands in the middle of Europe, and points.

"See? There it is."

"No, I don't," Jenny admits after a beat. "Are you sure it's real?"

"Oh, sorry. My finger was covering it," he replies, moving his admittedly large pointer finger slightly. "Do you see it now?"

And there it is. Snelgravia. Smaller than a grown man's pointer finger. And yet, somehow, Tom stands to rule over it all. No wonder he never invited me to brunch with his parents when they were in town, Jenny thinks. And then, immediately after, Oh my god, my fiancé is embarrassed of me. And also, no wonder he can afford such a nice place without a job.

 If Jenny decides to go to Snelgravia with Tom, turn to the trumpet on page 64.

 If Jenny decides she's not up for this whole "prince" thing, turn to the house on page 20.

BUILD YOUR OWN ROMANTIC COMEDY

"We've been together for a long time now," Tom tells Jenny. "And while I *can* imagine my life without you—"

Jenny begins to object when Tom replies, "It doesn't look even 1 percent as full and happy as it does with you in it," he continues. "Will you make me the happiest man on Earth by marrying me?"

He pulls out from his pocket and subsequently opens a tiny blue box—yes, Tiffany blue, because the ring is from Tiffany, of course—to reveal a beautiful, sparkling engagement ring.

"Is that a diamond, or an asteroid?" a blue-haired little old lady sitting nearby quips.

"Yes! Yes. Of course I'll marry you," Jenny says.

Jenny and Tom kiss.

The entire restaurant claps. The maître d' approaches, popping a bottle of their finest champagne.

"Thank god," the old woman says. "Because if you didn't say yes, I would have." Jenny and Tom both laugh.

"I have to call my parents! They are going to be over the moon," Jenny says, and begins to dig out her phone from her purse. But Tom just sits there.

"Don't you...also have to call your parents?" Jenny asks.

"Well, think about the time difference. I don't want to wake them."

"I think their only son's engagement to his beautiful, long-term girlfriend is a good enough reason to get them out of bed in the middle of the night. Unless they don't know you have a long-term girlfriend," Jenny says, laughing, because the idea of Tom's parents not even knowing of her existence simply must be a joke.

Tom just sits there.

"Do your parents...not know about me?" Jenny asks, enraged. "How?"

"It never came up?" Tom jokes, attempting to break the tension. It does not work.

 If Jenny is so mad she stabs Tom in the hand, turn to the hand on page 35.

 If Tom has a reasonable explanation for all of this, turn to the sofa on page 24.

"I think we should break up," Dave tells Jenny.

"Yes!" Jenny replies immediately, practically screaming.

"Great, so you agree. You think we should break up."

"You think we should break up" certainly doesn't sound anything like "I think we should have a May wedding and my parents already agreed to pay for the whole thing."

"Break up?" Jenny replies, confused.

"Yeah, I said we should break up and you agreed. I mean, I've felt like things have been off between us for months now, but I didn't think you felt the same way."

"Oh. Right," Jenny replies, crestfallen.

"What a relief!" Dave says, laughing. "I was expecting food thrown, eyes gouged," he continues, holding up his fingers to indicate exactly what an eye gouging would look like.

Jenny is crushed. Beyond crushed. Obliterated. "Since we're broken up, we can go halfsies on this, right?" Dave asks, before digging his phone out of his pocket. "Oh, I hope you don't mind," he says, indicating to his cell phone, "If I leave now, I can still go catch the game at Steve's." He smiles widely. "I always knew what a cool, chill girl you were."

 If Jenny then stabs Dave in the hand, turn to the hand on page 35.

 If Jenny considers going back home, heartbroken, turn to the house on page 20.

 If Jenny has to get back to working undercover at the mayor's office, turn to the magnifying glass on page 30.

 If Jenny is determined to make Dave jealous, turn to the apples on page 28.

"Hey, I got Chinese food," Jenny's boyfriend, Dave, calls out as she walks through the door. He's firmly planted on the worn-in loveseat in the small, boxy apartment they share, surrounded by white cartons of takeout.

Jenny kicks off her heels and joins him on the couch, unable to even summon the energy to retrieve her sweatpants from their bedroom closet.

"Steamed chicken and broccoli with, yes, soy sauce on the side," Dave says as he hands her a carton of food, anticipating her next question as to whether or not he had, in fact, remembered to order her soy sauce on the side.

"You're the best," Jenny replies, snatching the carton from him and nestling into his chest. She only then registers what's playing on the TV in front of them.

"You started watching without me?!" Jenny asks in disbelief, pulling away from Dave. They'd been binging *The Bleakest Night* for months now and had solemnly sworn not to watch it without the other.

"I'm sorry! I really wanted to see if this is the episode where Detective Mann finally avenges his dead wife, just like he kept saying he would! I'll rewind to the beginning."

"Yeah, you'd better," Jenny counters, comfortably settling back into her man's arms. He kisses her on top of the head.

"Could you imagine needing anything more than this?" Dave asks.

"No...I can't," Jenny answers, unsure if she means it, or even can begin to comprehend the question in the first place.

 If Jenny is considering getting out of Dodge and going back to her hometown, turn to the house on page 20.

 If Jenny's boyfriend dumps her, turn to the broken heart on page 26.

Saturday morning. The local farmer's market—the place where you can find every young professional in the region, if they aren't too hungover. Women clad in leggings inspect produce for its freshness while small children pull their parents' arms toward the baked goods stands.

"It's far too early to be outside. What are we doing outside? Do other people know how early it is?" Tom asks, shoving his aviator sunglasses onto his face.

"Stop! I already told you—they'll definitely be here," Jenny replies, leading Tom toward a veal and poultry stand. "And when *my* ex, Dave, discovers that I'm dating *you* and *your* ex, Natasha, discovers that you're dating *me*, they'll be so jealous they'll break up and get back together with us immediately."

Jenny paused to consider how many Toms, Daves, and Natashas there were in the world, relative to how many there were in her life, but before she could reflect too deeply, she heard Tom's voice asking:

"This whole fake dating thing? You really think they'll buy it?"

"We can say we found solace in each other's arms," Jenny assures him.

"But we don't have to like...touch, right? Because...gross."

"Rude," Jenny replies, offended. "Wait, look, there they are!"

There they were, indeed. Less than an organic, freshly baked loaf of pumpernickel bread's throw away stood Their Exes. A couple. Laughing, smiling, holding hands in what you could only classify as a flagrant display of public affection.

"Oh my god, they see us. They see us and they are coming over," Tom tells Jenny, jabbing her in the shoulder.

"Put your hand in my back pocket! Quick!" Tom doesn't have a chance to object—The Exes are upon them—and so into Jenny's back pocket his hand goes.

"Wow, so...you two are a thing now too then?" Tom's ex, Natasha, asks, surveying them skeptically.

"Sometimes love finds you when you least expect it. I mean you guys know a thing or two about that, right?" Jenny replies, eyeing Dave carefully and fantasizing about pelting him with tomatoes—the big kind, not those little grape tomatoes. Is throwing fruit a felony, or a misdemeanor? Somehow it's never come up on *Law and Order* before, so Jenny has no idea.

"Well, we should all get dinner sometime!" Natasha declares loudly, her voice climbing three octaves and reaching a pitch so high it could crack windows. "Follow me on Instagram and I'll follow you back! I'm sure you guys have lots of cute couple pics for me to fave."

"We should get going. It was good to see you," Dave says, and finally, after what feels like a millennium, their nightmare encounter at the farmer's market is over.

"So should we take a couples selfie on my phone or yours?" Tom asks, finally resigned to this new way of life.

Jenny pulls out her iPhone and holds the camera in front of their faces. "Say 'goals!'"

 If Jenny and Tom start spending more time together, turn to the bicycle on page 79.

 If Jenny and Tom have a night out and then get caught in the rain, turn to the rain cloud on page 81.

Jenny has been waiting over 20 minutes now for her interview to be the mayor's new secretary. But she doesn't mind. Those 20 minutes in the hallway outside the mayor's office give her extra time to go over all of her "qualifications" as to why *she* would be the ultimate assistant for a first-term boy-wonder mayor—not to mention, to review her fake-ish identity. Same schooling, same go-getter attitude, but with a different name (borrowed from her cousin) and, most importantly, a disguise: a pair of thick-framed black glasses—in case the boy wonder mayor happens to read her Politi-Bitch column.

"The mayor will see you now," says his chief of staff, Lorelei, emerging from the mayor's office. Jenny follows Lorelei inside to a tastefully decorated office, replete with a wood-burning fireplace and lots of maps on the walls. Why are men so into maps? Jenny ponders. Maybe I can write a column about that next. And there he sits, completely absorbed in a blueprint on his desk.

"Mr. Mayor, we have another candidate here to interview for the assistant position," Lorelei announces. And still, the mayor does not lift his head from the blueprint.

"I swear, I leave him alone for one second," Lorelei tells Jenny. "Mr. Mayor?" Finally, he snaps out of his reverie and stands to greet Jenny. He holds out his hand to her. She shakes it. He has a great handshake, she thinks. Firm grip. Nice, big hands too. But, of course, that's the observant journalist inside her. She can't help but notice even the smallest of details. It's not her fault, you see.

Jenny follows Lorelei inside to a tastefully decorated office, replete with a wood-burning fireplace and lots of maps on the walls. Why are men so into maps?

"I'll leave you two to talk," Lorelei announces, promptly exiting the room. Jenny takes a seat in front of the mayor, who she can't help but notice looks more like an actor who would play a mayor in a movie than an actual mayor himself. Those are the objective facts, and a journalist's job is to state the objective facts.

Jenny hands the mayor her résumé, but he swats it away. "I'm not interested in your qualifications," he tells her.

"Excuse me?" she replies. She put a lot of thought into this fake résumé. It deserves to be read.

"I'm sure they're great. What I'm more interested in is someone who has passion, who wants to make this city a better place. This will be far more than your typical executive assistant job. So, what do you say?" He asks with a smile, making Jenny, against her better instincts, a very happy constituent.

"I do," Jenny replies. "I mean, I'm in."

You are a journalist. You are a kickass journalist. You are the kind of journalist who can go undercover and lie about who you are for the sake of getting a good story.

It's a long mantra, but that's the mantra that Jenny has repeated to herself for the last seven years any time she's had to go undercover to tell the kind of story she wanted to. The kind of story she used to dream about telling when she was a kid. Real journalism that brings truth to power and improves the lives of the everyman. But this time was different.

One month later, Jenny stands outside the door to the mayor's office, waiting for him to call out "Come in!" which he usually does in a fairly cheery voice, no matter how stressed he is that day.

She knocked three times on the door to the mayor's office and waited for him to call out "Come in!" which he usually does in a fairly cheery voice, no matter how stressed he is that day. Jenny can now gauge his stress levels based on how much of his pencil he's chewed on that day—his vice, as he calls it, which just happens to be the same as hers.

When Jenny enters the office, she finds the mayor reclining in his chair, feet up on his desk, gnawing desperately on his pencil and reading what appears to be a very thick and very official document.

"Do you want to go over your day?" Jenny asks. "Or do you need some more time?"

"No, no, now is fine. I was just looking over some proposals for the downtown rezoning project. What's on the agenda for today?"

"You have a call with the head of the city council, a budget meeting, and you're scheduled to appear at the opening of that new floor of the children's hospital."

"Oh god, those photo ops. I'm awful at them. Will you come with me?"

"Sir, I don't know—"

"I told you to call me Tom," says the mayor, known to Jenny, per his wishes, (and his friends and family too, most likely) as *Tom*.

"Well...*Tom*," Jenny says, as if she were sounding out a word of a different language, "I just want to make sure that's something within my job bounds."

"Of course. And it'll be helpful for me to have someone there in case I get someone's name wrong or accidentally forget my lines."

"You don't really have lines, do you?"

"What do you think I have those speechwriters for?" Tom says with a sly grin. "But seriously, you're my assistant, it's fine."

"Great, looking forward to it."

Three hours later, with Tom conveniently held up at a deadlocked budget meeting, Jenny is back in his office—but this time, she is alone. And she's snooping.

Jenny has a 5- to 15-minute window to find that document Tom was holding earlier, the one about downtown rezoning. Because Jenny has a more than just sneaking suspicion that lots of the proposals for the project will involve razing historical landmarks and putting up high-rise condos. In this moment, she vaguely remembers that she's overdue to respond to a text from her best friend, CJ, but she pushes that thought away. "Focus, Jenny, focus," she tells herself.

Jenny pokes around the room, opening Tom's desk drawers, checking underneath political science tomes and no fewer than five Theodore Roosevelt biographies, and only comes upon scores of chewed-up pencils. Against every single one of her better instincts, she grabs one of the destroyed pencils by the eraser and brings it level with her eyeline to examine it more closely.

"Gross," Jenny can't help but say aloud.

"What's gross?" Tom asks from the doorway, where he's somehow magically appeared.

Panicked, Jenny chucks the pencil across the room.

"I know, I know. It's a terrible habit," he says, entering the room. "The chief put you up to this, huh?"

"Guilty as charged," Jenny replies, lying. The proposals will have to wait.

"Oh my god, I can't find the mayor" is not a sentence Jenny ever thought she'd say to herself, but she also never thought she'd find herself holding his chewed-up pencil in her hands either, so there's a lot of the unexpected happening today.

Almost immediately after they arrive at Stern Carson Hospital, Jenny immediately loses sight of Tom. After spending an hour staking out all of the biggest donors in the city—the most elbow-rubbing worthy of the bunch—Jenny finally gives up.

BUILD YOUR OWN ROMANTIC COMEDY

She wanders into a corridor to try to find a bathroom or maybe even a vending machine, when she happens upon Tom, rubbing elbows not with the upper echelon of society but instead with some of the hospital's smallest patients.

Tom, the youngest mayor of the city since the city's first leader passed away and his child bride secretly ran the city for six months, sits cross-legged on the floor, racing toy cars with a small boy. A young girl has painted a butterfly on his face.

When he sees Jenny, he smiles and says, "Now these, these are my people."

Jenny has a feeling that digging up dirt on the mayor is going to take a little bit longer than she thought.

 For Jenny to meet Tom's girlfriend, turn to the mug on page 59.

 To see things from CJ's perspective for a bit, turn to the plate on page 39.

 Want to skip ahead to Jenny writing her article and Tom getting mad about it? Turn to the typewriter on page 102.

Chapter Four

GAGS

Jenny picks up a fork on the table and stabs her boyfriend in the hand!

Blood spurts out of his hand, squirting everywhere. So shocked by the sight of the blood—not to mention the fact that it was Jenny who stabbed him in the first place—he passes out. A nearby waitress rushes over, hoping to contain the blood by turning a bunch of cloth napkins into a tourniquet, but she passes out too.

Jenny, in complete disbelief that her boyfriend's actions have driven her to stab him in the hand with a fork like he's a baked potato, also passes out. And in her last moment of clarity, Jenny thinks to herself, "Looks like I'm going to be late for work tomorrow."

 If Jenny, now on the lam, goes back to her hometown, turn to the house on page 20.

 If you want Jenny to be the owner of a coffee shop/bakery/bookstore, turn to the coffee cup on page 6.

Jenny can't remember the last time she slept for more than three hours a night. She walks the streets at all hours in a daze, wearing mismatched clothes, thinking only of her job and work. Nothing but her job and work.

She ignores calls from friends. Even texts from her mom, whom she's never ignored.

Work is the most important thing. You need that promotion, she tells herself.

One day, after what feels like years, she bumps into Tom on the street.

"Hey, Jenny!" he calls, happy to see her.

"Should I stop and speak to him?" Jenny asks herself, but then she remembers her job—the true love of her life. No one can make me as happy as my job can, she remembers. My job won't break my heart. My job won't ignore my texts. My job won't make me go to potlucks with his boring friends from college who never make enough food. So she keeps walking.

What could've been, they both think.

 If Jenny has a change of heart and she and Tom start to spend time together again, turn to the bicycle on page 79.

 To see things from CJ's perspective, turn to the plate on page 39.

Jenny is on Cloud Nine. After spending (a number she isn't willing to say aloud) years looking for the right guy—finally, *finally* she has found him. And she's pretty sure— no, *absolutely positive*—that he feels the same way about her.

Tom and Jenny have spent a lazy, romantic day at the park, when finally it's time for them to pack up their picnic items and head home.

Nearby, a group of vaguely twenty- to thirty-something men throw a Frisbee around, their tan, muscular backs glistening in the day's perfect sunlight. Not long ago, Jenny would right that very moment have been surmising the best way to strike up a conversation with these Frisbee devotees. But those days are behind her.

"Hey! Catch!" Jenny hears in the distance. She looks up, only to find the men's Frisbee careening toward her. What the hell? she thinks. She can still play ball—or Frisbee, that is.

She leaps aerodynamically toward the Frisbee, catching it triumphantly in her hand. A moment of victory.

She's never caught a Frisbee before. Unfortunately, in her effort to grab hold of the flying disc, Jenny fails to see the corgi–dachshund mix below her.

Her ankles catch the dog, her knees buckling. Bone by bone, every single one of her limbs hits the hard, completely solid ground.

"Ow," she says.

Four hours and a cocktail of pain medications later, Jenny finds herself waiting to see the ER doctor, her entire body wrapped in casting.

"I am so sorry to tell you this...Ms....Jenny...but you have broken every single bone in your body," the doctor reports some time later, sounding, well, genuinely very sorry.

The important thing though, is that for once in her life, she caught the Frisbee. And she plans to tell him just that...right after she regains feeling in her jaw.

If Jenny and Tom head to an antiques fair, turn to the boat on page 56.

 To see how Tom sees things, turn to the baseball on page 87.

Tom, Tom, Tom. All CJ ever hears Jenny talk about anymore is Tom.

They are sitting at brunch, picking at their egg white omelets, Jenny the entire time talking about Tom and all of her many, many complex feelings about him.

Every once in a while, CJ chimes in and says, "Did he *really* say that?" or, "You are so much better than him," or "Oh my god, yucky!"—her signature phrase.

> CJ sighs deeply, imagining what it would be like if she weren't the sidekick for once.

CJ sighs deeply, imagining what it would be like if she weren't the sidekick for once. If they talked about her hopes, her dreams. Her deep yearning to start wearing more intricate patterns. Her desire to learn how to play the mandolin. Her crush on her boss whom she was already sleeping with.

"CJ? CJ?" Jenny calls out to her, pulling CJ out of her reverie. "These egg whites, they taste a little off, don't they?"

"Oh my god, yucky!" CJ replies, and with that, Jenny is placated. She launches into another tirade about Tom.

The mandolin would have to wait.

To see how Tom sees things, turn to the baseball on page 87.

For a quick Jenny-and-Tom-spending-time-together montage, turn to the bicycle on page 79.

Jenny has had enough. She's sick of Natasha's backhanded compliments, her snarky comments, her not-so-veiled attempts to get between Jenny and Tom. When Jenny hears Natasha make yet another crack about her clothes, saying "It's so impressive how you can find outfits that highlight your body type," Jenny knows she can't hold her rage in any longer.

Before she can even think about what she's doing—or the fact that they're on the street in broad daylight—she balls her hand up into a fist and brings it as far back behind her as it can go. Her fist hurtles through space—with everyone's eyes on it— until it makes contact with Natasha's nose.

Crack.

Natasha stumbles backward. A trickle of blood begins to drip down past her lips to her chin. Natasha quickly touches her face, where she discovers the blood and something very seriously wrong with her nose.

"You broke my nose, you freak!" she exclaims.

In an amazing show of synchronicity, everyone around them begins to clap and chant, "Jenny! Jenny! Jenny!" Even complete strangers. Tom smiles and says, "That's my girl."

They hoist her on their shoulders and carry her on a victory march.

Jenny, the hero.

 Time for a high school flashback! Turn to the beer bottle on page 85.

 Is Natasha really as bad as she seems? Turn to the ice cream cone on page 61.

Jenny and Tom are enjoying a beautiful Snelgravian day, strolling the castle grounds, when suddenly the Snelgravian secretary of defense and the prime minister come sprinting toward them with dire looks on their faces.

"Whoa, whoa, where's the fire?" Tom asks.

"In the Snelgravian woods, I'm afraid. Snelgravia is at war."

Tom grimaces. He didn't expect the answer to involve a literal fire.

"What? But Snelgravia is a peaceful nation!"

"*Was* a peaceful nation," the prime minister corrects Tom.

"How did this happen?"

"Well, you know how you said not to disturb you, no matter what it was because you were really busy with Jenny and that was the most important thing in the world to you, more important than official Snelgravian business? And that whatever it was, we could handle it?"

Jenny can't help but be moved by this. "Aw, sweetie."

"Yes..." Tom concedes.

"As it turns out, we couldn't handle it. We couldn't handle it at all," the secretary of defense says before crossing herself.

"We need you to come to the War Room immediately," the prime minister adds.

Unsure what to do, Tom searches Jenny's face desperately for approval.

"Go! Go to the War Room. I'll be here...whenever you're done."

"I hope we all are," the prime minister says gravely, "I hope we all are."

 Jenny isn't so sure she can handle this. Turn to the airplane on page 118.

"Needless to say, I am very, very disappointed," Cynthia tells Jenny, peering at her intently from behind her desk.

Jenny sits quietly in front of her boss, hands folded on her lap. She awaits her opportunity to apologize and to throw herself at Cynthia's feet, begging for mercy.

"This is a huge breach of journalistic ethics and I simply cannot have this from my staff," Cynthia says in a firm whisper, which everyone knows is much scarier than yelling. "I know what's going on between you and the mayor, Jenny. I know about your feelings for him," her utter disdain for love and its corresponding emotions growing increasingly clear. "A female journalist falling in love with her subject? You are an embarrassment not only to the profession of journalism, but women everywhere. Pack up your things. I want you out of here by 5 p.m. The sight of you sickens me."

Jenny swallows hard and steels herself to say, "I just want to say—"

"Say what? That you put your romantic interests ahead of your career ambitions? That what I do—what *we*—do here is completely frivolous to you? You silly little girl. I bet you think you'll just march out of here and get another job at some other newspaper or magazine or maybe even at the local *TV* station. I want you to know that I will personally ensure that you will never—*never*—find work in this town—or any other—as a journalist ever again. Leave now."

And just like that, Cynthia turns her attention back to her computer, dismissing Jenny as quickly as she would a sentence that ends in a preposition.

Years and years of hard work undone, just like that.

What now?

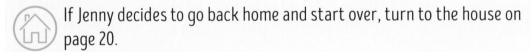

If Jenny decides to go back home and start over, turn to the house on page 20.

If Jenny needs her mom—and her advice—turn to the pillow on page 111.

If Jenny apologizes to Tom in a big way, turn to the flower on page 117.

Chapter Five

RELATIONSHIP BUILDING

When Tom asked Jenny to meet him at an address she didn't recognize, and to "wear comfortable clothes," she didn't quite know what to expect. That he was going to murder her, maybe, and that he wanted her to dress comfortably so that it would be a fair fight.

Thankfully, that isn't the case. He has something much more sadistic in mind: rock climbing.

An hour after arriving, Jenny finds herself in a position she never thought she would: 30 feet in the air, pressed against a wall, holding on for dear life.

"You can relax, you're wearing a harness, and Karl down there has you on belay. Nothing's going to happen to you," Tom calls out from above, scaling his way to the high heavens, or at the very least, the ceiling.

"Easy for you to say," Jenny mutters.

Tom rappels down to meet her. "I see the problem. You're too tense. If you relax, you'll get more blood flow in your fingers, and you can grab on more easily."

"What, are you like a rock-climbing guru?" Jenny asks.

"Not a guru," Tom says, "but I miss being in the mountains, and rock climbing here…it's the closest I feel to home. And it helps me to relax and unwind."

"And here I thought you used alcohol and picking up women for that," Jenny tells him, taken aback.

"Well, it doesn't hurt," Tom replies, "but I don't do nearly as much of that as you'd think."

"Still waiting for the right girl, huh?" Jenny asks, teasing him.

"More waiting for her to decide I'm the right guy," he tells her with a knowing glance.

> *Could he mean me? Jenny asks herself. Surely, no. If he did then why would he be so vague about it?*

Could he mean me? Jenny asks herself. Surely, no. If he did then why would he be so vague about it? Jenny meets Tom's eye for a moment and then breaks away. She clears her throat, easing the tension.

"I think I'm getting the hang of this climbing thing. Race you to the top?"

To get a glimpse of how Tom sees things, turn to the baseball on page 87.

 Is there another guy in the picture for Jenny? Turn to the bar sign on page 62 to find out.

"That'll be $25.50," the pizza guy tells Jenny. She hands him the money and returns to the conference room, where she finds Tom ripping out pages from old issues of *Woman* magazine.

"Two pizza pies, one pepperoni for me, one veggie for you, three bags of sour cream and onion chips, two liters of Sprite, brownies my mom made, actually, and a giant glass full of Swedish Fish I stole from the start-up downstairs," Jenny says, listing out all of the junk food she and Tom have selected to power them through an all-nighter.

"Hey, don't forget about this," he says, pulling out a fifth of Jack Daniel's.

"Alcohol? *Here*?" Jenny asks in disbelief.

"Please, like this place didn't run on cocaine in the '80s. This is the best way to appease the magazine gods."

Jenny shakes her head. "You are too much."

"Or am I just enough?"

"Plenty of time to figure that out later," Jenny says. "But right now, let's get to work."

8 P.M.

Jenny and Tom sit in complete silence, each eating a slice of pizza.

"This pizza is good," Tom says.

"Yeah, I ordered it from the place around the corner," Jenny replies.

"Cool." He pauses. "I usually go to the place down the street."

9 P.M.

Jenny and Tom each pore over their notes from the audience surveys the research team conducted, still in silence.

Tom looks around the table, searching for something.

"Hey, are there any more of those Swedish Fish?"

Jenny, who has just bitten the head off the last one, holds the remainder of the Swedish Fish's body out to Tom, offering it to him.

He shakes his head.

"Your loss."

11 P.M.

"OK, I can't do this sober anymore," Tom says, breaking out the bottle of whiskey and pouring it—neat—into an empty cup.

Jenny tsks disapprovingly.

"Fine, I'll pour you some too."

To hell with it, Jenny thinks. What's the worst that could happen?

1 A.M.

"I should've gotten more—*hiccup*—snacks," Jenny says. Oh no, she's hiccupping. Certainly not a sign of sobriety, least of all hers.

"Hey! Don't deflect the question—it's your turn!"

"Ok, *truth*."

"Of course you picked truth."

"What's that supposed to mean?"

"It means that you like to play it safe! This whole magazine does."

How and why she came to be drunk and playing Truth or Dare with a man she loathes is suddenly of no importance to Jenny. Because in that moment, she has *an idea*. A good one.

"Oh my god, that's it!" Jenny exclaims, getting up and walking out of the room.

"What's it?" Tom calls after her. "What?" But she's not there anymore, nor can she hear him.

"I hate when people do that," he laments.

3 A.M.

"You really think this will work?" Tom asks Jenny, sounding, for the first time since she's met him, a bit unsure of himself.

They're standing over the presentation they spent the last two hours putting together, almost in awe at the fact that they managed—really, *she* managed—to actually pull something together.

"Well, if it doesn't, I'm out of a job. You too, probably."

"Hey, no way am I letting you drag me down with you, so that means this *has* to work. But what we *should* do," he says, pulling out *another* bottle of whiskey from underneath the table, "is celebrate."

And this time, Jenny doesn't protest at all.

5 A.M.

Jenny can't remember exactly what was so funny, but she knows she can't stop laughing. Neither can Tom. Nor can she bring herself to get up from the couch they're sitting on in the conference room.

"Look, the sun's coming up," Tom says, gesturing to the window. Indeed, the sun is beginning to shine, casting a new light on the conference room, among other things.

"Hey, we never finished our game," Jenny tells Tom. "And I think it was my turn."

"OK, truth or dare?"

"Dare," Jenny says, inching closer to Tom until they finally kiss.

"That's not what I was going to dare you to do, but I'll take it," Tom says, before leaning in to kiss Jenny again.

 Does Jenny nail her presentation? Turn to the woman on page 107 to find out.

 To see Jenny debrief the incident to CJ, turn to the stationary bike on page 73.

 If Jenny gets so wrapped in work she forgets about Tom, turn to the hourglass on page 36.

 BUILD YOUR OWN ROMANTIC COMEDY

"I can't believe *this* is your car," Jenny tells Tom as he pulls up in front of her brownstone—of which the exterior alone is beautiful and historic—at 10 a.m. on the dot.

"Believe it," he calls out from the driver's seat of his beat-up, once-cherry red '92 Chevy Camaro, its incredibly dusty windows rolled down.

"Don't you have enough money for a new car?" Jenny asks, throwing way too many bags in the backseat and very hesitantly climbing into the passenger seat, which, yep, is sticky.

"First of all, we live in New York City. It'd be incredibly impractical to buy a new car. Second, this is my Old Faithful. She's never let me down—which is more than I can say for any *human* woman," Tom says.

"Gross. Well, all *she* has to do is take us about three hours north so that we can meet everyone at the Farm Retreat this weekend, and get us safely home in a few days. Can she do that?" Jenny asks, emphasizing the gender pronoun Tom has given his car to show him how stupid she thinks he, and by extension, his car, is.

"She can do all that and more," Tom replies, punctuating his sentence with a wink.

"Good, because whoever gets to the Farm Retreat last gets the least yeast for their sourdough starter. How embarrassing." She shudders at the thought. "Can we get some music for the ride, at least?"

"You bet we can," Tom replies, pressing play on his stereo, and with that motion he summons the opening guitar lick of The Rolling Stones' seminal hit "Beast of Burden."

"The Rolling Stones? You are so predictable," Jenny tells Tom, rolling her eyes accordingly. But he's too busy bopping his head to the song to hear her. And with a slam of his foot on the gas pedal, they're on their way.

That is, until an hour later—miles away from the city and conveniently close to nothing—when Old Faithful is sputtering steam from her front hood.

Jenny nods her way through a phone conversation with AAA, furious with Tom and his car, and with herself for accepting a ride with him in the first place.

Meanwhile, Tom futzes around with Not So Faithful Anymore, accomplishing nothing.

"AAA says they can send someone tomorrow," Jenny tells Tom as she hangs up the phone. "So you should probably stop doing...whatever it is that you're doing to your car. I don't think she likes it. Maybe you don't know what's under that hood as well as you thought." Jenny laughs, because, of course, she's not really talking about the car at all.

"I swear this has never happened before," Tom says, pulling his head out from under the hood and revealing a thick streak of grease across his forehead. And while, sure, if someone else saw Tom, a grown man, dirty from changing a car, chances are that person might find him attractive, but Jenny, most certainly, would not.

"This is just great. This retreat was my chance to prove myself to Cynthia, and now she'll never take me seriously. All thanks to you and your stupid car."

"Hey, don't blame me! You accepted the ride," Tom counters.

"Oh, so this is *my* fault somehow?" Jenny folds her arms and turns away from Tom, wishing she had taken the train or made even one life decision that would have led her on a different path entirely.

"Hey, it looks like there's a motel up ahead a little bit. Let's cool off there and reassess in the morning."

She desperately does not want to spend a night in some probably awful motel, in God knows where, with a man she hates. But what's her other choice? Stand on the side of the road all night to prove a point?

"Fine. But we're getting our own rooms."

And at that, Tom smirks. "I never suggested otherwise."

 If Tom and Jenny spend the night together, turn to the bed on page 53.

 To see Jenny debrief the incident to CJ, turn to the stationary bike on page 73.

 If Tom and Jenny embrace their musical side, turn to the music note on page 89.

Her entire life, Jenny was not someone who was ever at a loss for words. "Verbose" is how her 10th-grade English teacher put it. "You talk too much" is what one of her not-so-nice ex-boyfriends used to say.

But when Jenny sees the Newport, Rhode Island, manse that her doppelgänger grew up in—the house that now belongs to her—the only words she can come up with are "Oh my god" and she says them over and over again, from when her chauffeured black town car pulls up in front of the gorgeous estate (with pillars! it has pillars!), throughout her tour of its 25 rooms (bedrooms, living rooms, bowling alley rooms, all kinds of rooms), and up to and including the moment when she discovers the mansion's library, replete with a first-edition copy of Jane Austen's *Pride and Prejudice*.

> Her entire life, Jenny was not someone who was ever at a loss for words. "Verbose" is how her 10th-grade English teacher put it. "You talk too much" is what one of her not-so-nice ex-boyfriends used to say.

Slowly, carefully, Jenny pulls it off the shelf and holds it in her hands, as carefully as she would hold a tiny baby, or one of those infinity stones from those Avengers movies everyone is always talking about.

"Oh my god," she says aloud, deeply breathing in the smell of the books, in disbelief and amazement that this, somehow, was her life now.

"It's pretty incredible, isn't it?" a voice calls out behind her. Jenny whips around, mentally preparing herself to answer any question she has to about her doppelgänger's life, where she's been the last five years, and why she's close to tears in the most beautiful library she's ever seen. But when she sees *him*, his twinkling green eyes, his Crest-sponsored smile, all of that disappears from her brain.

"Oh my god."

"I know, it's something isn't it?" he asks.

"Something, indeed," Jenny replies, still at a loss for words.

"The last time I saw you, you told me you wanted to get rid of all of these 'dusty' books to make way for a spa."

What kind of a monster would do that? Jenny asks herself, before remembering that to all of these people, *she's* that monster.

"Well, you know what they say, time and ashrams change people."

"That's true, they do say that," Tom says, with a laugh. "My mother—you know, Cecilia—she told me about your partial memory loss. I'm so sorry."

"Thank you, I'm adjusting to life all right. So, what are we? Were we?" Jenny asks, hoping Tom will say "husband and wife," "fiancés," or "lovers." She would even accept "two people who never speak but kiss each other on the mouth every full moon. It's part of an ancient ritual, don't worry about it."

"Friends. Good friends. I mean, to be honest, I always had a huge crush on you, but you never gave me the time of day," he says with a shy smile, breaking their eye contact.

Jenny smiles back. She has a feeling her schedule is suddenly going to clear up.

 To see Jenny spend time with Tom in Newport, turn to the boat on page 56.

 If Jenny gets into an unfortunate Frisbee accident, turn to the Frisbee on page 37.

BUILD YOUR OWN ROMANTIC COMEDY

When Jenny wakes up in the morning, she can't stop smiling. Her grin is as wide as her face as she remembers everything that had happened the night before. Her night with *Tom*. What a perfect name. What a perfect night! She can't wait to say it over and over again.

But when she turns over in bed, expecting to find Tom's sleeping, perfect face in front of hers, he's nowhere to be found. His side of the bed is empty, and she doesn't hear the shower running. She even checks under the bed because who knows what guys are into these days. It seems like it's changing all the time.

> *She even checks under the bed because who knows what guys are into these days.*

Did he think last night was horrible? she thinks. Did I make a huge mistake? My god, I really need a cup of coffee.

And then another impossible but horrific thought flashes into Jenny's head: Am I bad at sex?

How often do men spontaneously disintegrate immediately after intercourse? Jenny would like to see the stats.

She checks her phone—nothing from Tom—but three texts from CJ, absolutely demanding to know details and also suggesting they go to brunch at some place where you get to choose the chicken that produces your eggs.

Just when Jenny is about to pull on her clothes, drive to the airport, and move somewhere, anywhere—even Snelgravia, perhaps—Tom walks through the door, carrying two cups of coffee—scalding-hot, triple-shot, extra-large latte for her—and a bag teeming with pastries.

"You were asleep, and I didn't want to wake you," Tom tells Jenny, before kissing her and handing over her coffee.

And with that, Jenny's wide smile is back on her face. She has a feeling it is going to stay there all day long.

If Jenny catches Tom with (gasp) another woman, turn to the purse on page 90.

 Wait—has Jenny been lying to everyone about who she is? Is she about to get caught? Turn to the sunglasses on page 100 to find out.

BUILD YOUR OWN ROMANTIC COMEDY

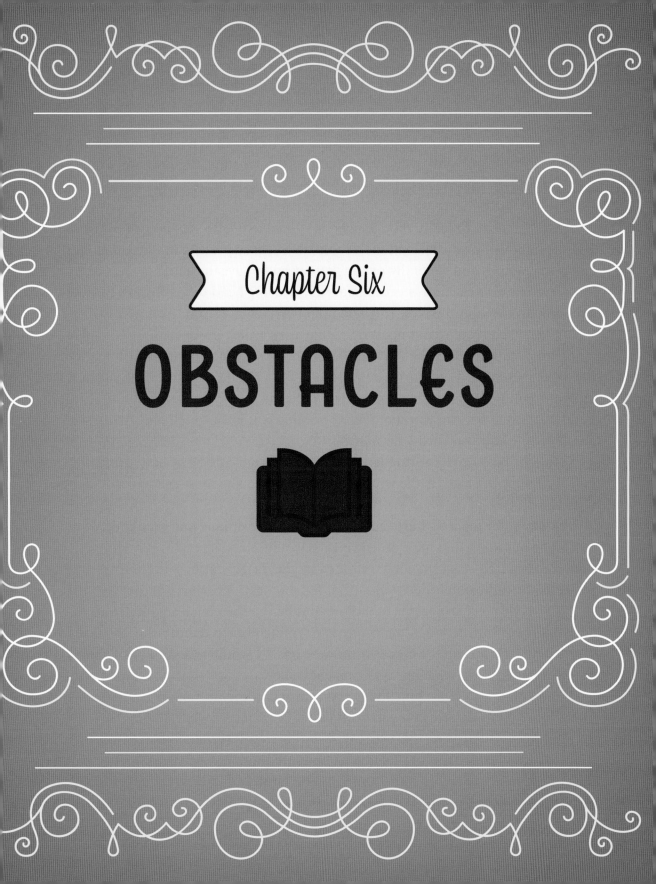

Chapter Six

OBSTACLES

The Newport Antique Fair is, perhaps for some, a chance to go antiquing and pick up a new Victorian-era fainting couch for their foyer or a stained-glass lamp from 1929 (yes, the specific year *does* matter). But for the crème de la crème of Newport, it's a place to see and be seen.

This is all news to Jenny though, who is still adjusting to the lifestyle of the rich and the famous—or the rich, at the very least. She was pretty sure she heard Cecilia call being famous and generally seeking attention "nouveau riche."

When she arrives, Tom is waiting for her, wearing head to toe Brooks Brothers and looking every bit the New England prep boy he was raised to be.

"Wow, where's your boat docked?" Jenny asks as he approaches.

"In the harbor, why?" he answers, before realizing that she's razzing him. "Oh, the outfit. Yes, well, as embarrassing as this is for a grown man to admit, my mother picked it out. Believe me, this is not how I prefer to dress. You seem so different from how you used to be. Are you sure there's nothing you want to tell me? About who you are, or even...how you spell your name?"

Could he be onto the truth? Jenny wonders. Should she be honest? No, Jenny tells herself. Telling the truth is the wrong thing to do, and she must keep up this charade until she dies.

As they enter the lot where the vendors tout their unique and rare finds, Jenny can't help but think that her doppelgänger's would-be boyfriend is very different than she expected—a suspicion confirmed by the dagger tattoo she glimpses on his perfectly formed bicep.

"Hey, is that —" she begins to inquire, but before she can, a very tall, and admittedly very attractive, woman comes storming over to them.

"Jenny," she squeals. "I'd heard you were back! I would've called but I simply did not believe it." She gives Jenny a kiss on each cheek.

"And Tom!" She grabs him and greets him accordingly. "I never heard from you after that night in Cabo. Have you been hiding from me or what?"

And while Tom *says* no, his eyes say, "Absolutely, oh my god, yes."

Now, Jenny has had a lot of catching up to do these last few weeks. How to dress, how to act, how to pretend to be someone else entirely, but this, this takes Jenny all of

30 seconds to fully comprehend. Instinctually she understands that this woman, who is probably named something like *Natasha*, likes Tom and that they shared at least one drunken night in Cabo (and who knows what else) and because Tom seemingly likes Jenny, that means Natasha hates her. It was as if it were written in the stars.

Before Jenny can grab Tom by the hand and whisk him toward some throw pillow that was on the *Titanic* or an opium pipe previously owned by Zelda Fitzgerald, she hears someone calling out her name.

"Jenny! Jenny!"

What random person from her doppelgänger's past could it be now?

But as the voice draws nearer, it turns out it's not someone from her doppelgänger's past—but someone from her own. CJ. They were bartenders together at Sleaze Palace, an upscale gastropub, in another lifetime.

"Wow, I never thought I'd see *you* here, Jenny—"

"Well, here I am!" Jenny says, cutting CJ off before she can say her last name. "I love antiques!"

Immediately, Natasha and Tom exchange confused looks. From what Jenny can gather, her doppelgänger *loves* antiques, and no one would be surprised to see her in what could only be considered her natural habitat.

"Who is this?" Natasha asks, clearly suspicious.

"My friend, CJ. We went to camp together," Jenny replies, grabbing the first thing that comes into her head and running with it.

"But you and I went to camp together, and I don't remember CJ," Natasha says, clearly loving this.

"Well, you *are* a little bit older than me, aren't you?" Jenny says through gritted teeth, desperately hoping that Natasha is, in fact, older than her. Miraculously, she is, and the comment shuts Natasha up. For a second, she has the upper hand and she uses it to tell Natasha and Tom, "Can you two give me a second to catch up with my friend—alone?"

And when CJ and Jenny are by themselves, and after making plans to continue seeing each other, Jenny recounts everything that's happened over the last few weeks: the mistaken identity, the money, the lies. CJ can't help but laugh. "Jenny, I always knew you were destined for something great."

If Jenny and Tom have a night out and get caught in the rain, turn to the rain cloud on page 81.

 If Jenny and Tom start spending more and more time together, turn to the bicycle on page 79.

By a number of measures (not her own, necessarily), Jenny is not a religious woman. But there is one ritual she holds absolutely sacred, and that is weekly happy hour at her favorite bar, Bonnie's, the one with the string lights that puts cute little paper umbrellas in your drinks. Plus, Bonnie's has the most important thing you could want in any drinking establishment you patronize: cheap, strong cocktails.

Jenny is on her third Moscow Mule when she spots Tom, the person she's been hoping to see walk through the door every time she happens to look at the entrance, maybe checking her phone every few seconds to see if he's sent her a text, and maybe the person she's been dropping hints to about this happy hour all week long. But she's calm. She's casual!

> *This is the moment of truth. Three Moscow Mules and one flirtatious touch deep, Jenny is ready to tell the object of her affection How She Feels.*

"Tom! You made it!" Jenny calls out to him, waving him over to her spot at the bar. He smiles back. It should be illegal to have a smile that nice, Jenny thinks. You could destabilize countries with that smile.

"I did! Thanks for the invite. And for the multiple text and email reminders."

"Well, I didn't want you to miss out on the glory that is happy hour at Bonnie's," Jenny tells him.

"I'll have a Moscow Mule," he tells the bartender.

"Hey! That's what I'm having," Jenny says, nudging him affectionately.

"Well, it's just one of the many things we have in common then," Tom replies, mussing Jenny's hair. (Of course, if anyone else even laid a finger on her head, it'd be lights out for them. But in this case, she's just happy he's touching her at all.)

This is it. This is the moment of truth. Three Moscow Mules and one flirtatious touch deep, Jenny is ready to tell the object of her affection How She Feels.

"Speaking of things we have in common..." Jenny starts, when Tom breaks their eye contact and starts waving manically.

"Yeah, I like waving," Jenny says and begins waving as well, mirroring his actions and thinking, "This is fun. This is good. I should wave my arms around more often."

"Natasha! Natasha, we're over here," Tom calls out to an impossibly tall, impossibly chic, impossibly good-looking woman. Even from a distance Jenny can tell her manicure is perfect. She doesn't have a single split end on her head. She even knows how to correctly apply lip liner. If she were a superhero, her moniker would be The Impossible. And then her and Tom's impossibly attractive family would be called, collectively, The Impossibles. They would use their good looks and keen fashion sense to coax nuclear codes away from villains.

Natasha walks toward them, and deep down Jenny knows exactly what's coming. Don't say it, don't say it, don't say it. But he does. And there's nothing she can do to stop him.

Noooooooooo.

"This is my girlfriend, Natasha."

 Oh no! Natasha and Tom break up and now she's dating...Dave. If Tom and Jenny start dating to make them jealous, turn to the apples on page 28.

 If Jenny embraces her outdoorsy side, turn to the mountains on page 44.

BUILD YOUR OWN ROMANTIC COMEDY

What does she have that I don't have? Natasha asks herself for what must be the umpteenth time, as she watches Tom and Jenny flit around and flirt happily, not a care in the world. And certainly, without a care for Natasha's feelings.

She and Tom had a real connection. At least that's what she'd thought before he became so taken with happy-go-lucky, wide-eyed Jenny, who hung onto every word he'd said like she'd never met a more intelligent or interesting person in her life. Please. It was all enough to make Natasha sick. Except she never got sick. She never allowed herself to. Getting sick was for weaklings, the Jennys of the world. Not for the Natashas, who ate sensibly, were constantly varying their workout routine, and remembered to take their multivitamin everyday. How many people out there can really say they remembered to take their multivitamin every single morning, no matter what came up that day, no matter where they found themselves? Natasha, for one, could.

And Natasha couldn't be blamed for thinking she and Tom had a real connection because those were the actual words he had said to her: "Natasha, you and I have a real connection."

She sighed as she watched Jenny get just a smidgen of ice cream on her nose and Tom lick it off. How perfectly adorable. She was laying out in the park, reading Karl Ove Knausgård, as she liked to do on a nice day, and clearly Jenny and Tom had a similar idea. Minus the Karl Ove Knausgård, of course. Natasha knew she could have her pick of any guy in this park. But that didn't matter. It was Tom she wanted.

Natasha knew she came off as difficult, abrasive. A bitch, maybe, even. But she knew she wouldn't luck her way into the right man or the right job, the way Jenny had. She was going to have to fight for Tom. And just like Detective Mann from that show the *The Bleakest Night*, when Natasha fought, she fought to win.

 If Jenny catches Tom kissing (ugh) Natasha, turn to the purse on page 90.

 If Natasha unmasks Jenny as her doppelganger Jennie, turn to the sunglasses on page 100.

Another night at Bonnie's, another night of Jenny nursing a Moscow Mule. All the regulars are there, a group she considers herself a part of. She has another three years, max, before her frequent, habitual patronage of this establishment becomes something of a problem, but for now she's safe. Before Jenny could ponder this too deeply, however, Tom is by her side, picking the maraschino cherry out of her drink and biting the fruit off its stem.

"Excuse me, that was extremely rude!" Jenny informs him as he pulls up a stool next to her.

"Hey, if you want something, you gotta go for it," he tells her before ordering his own Moscow Mule.

"You know, you're so right," she says picking the cherry out of the drink freshly placed in front of Tom, and putting it between her teeth, before kissing Tom square on the mouth.

"Wow," he says, as they break apart.

"I know, right?" Jenny replies, "I think Dave caught the whole thing," nodding her head toward the back of the bar, where Dave is, indeed, standing and watching them intently.

"I think he's coming over! Pretend like you enjoyed that," Jenny says quickly. Tom nods slowly, pretending like he has to pretend. *A lot of layers here.*

"Fancy seeing you guys here!" Dave remarks, his voice strained, as though he has something caught in the back of his throat.

"Well, you know this is my favorite bar," Jenny tells him.

"Yeah, *we* come here all the time," Tom adds, putting his hand on Jenny's knee. If he's going to do this, he might as well enjoy watching Dave squirm like a raver waiting for the beat to drop.

"Jenny, can I talk to you for a second?" Dave asks. "Alone." He gives Tom a withering look and Jenny has to bite her lip to keep from smiling.

"I'll be waiting," Tom says, before catching Jenny's face in another kiss.

Whoa, Tom is a really, really good kisser, Jenny thinks before stopping herself. Keep your eyes on the prize, Jenny. Dave is the guy. It's Dave, and it's been Dave all along.

In a small, deserted corner of the bar—one that's usually occupied by a rowdy birthday party or two college kids sucking face—Dave stares at Jenny intently, steeling himself as he says, "Jenny, I've been thinking about you a lot lately, and do you think we could go somewhere and talk more? I know you're with Tom now, but—"

It takes all the strength Jenny can muster to not burst out and scream "Finally!" or "I'd follow you to the ends of the Earth!" Instead she nods slowly, as if she's actually taking the time to weigh the meaning of his words.

"Yeah," she finally says, "I can do that." And with that, she follows Dave out the side door of Bonnie's, glancing back at Tom ordering another round of Moscow Mules at the bar. For a second—maybe even less than that—she feels a pang, something tight in her chest. But she swats it down and smiles at Dave. "Ready to go?"

 If Jenny goes home to Dave, her now-boyfriend, turn to the take-out box on page 27.

 If Jenny needs to debrief with CJ, turn to the stationary bike on page 73.

 If Tom confesses how he *really* feels about Jenny, turn to the duck on page 94.

"*This* is where you grew up?" Jenny says to Tom as they pull up in front of a gorgeous old house—nay, mansion—high in the verdant hills of Snelgravia.

"Well, I spent most of my childhood at boarding schools abroad, but yes, this is where the family debunks during our Christmases and summers," Tom replies.

He turns the car off and looks at Jenny intently.

"My family can be...a lot. So, if at any point you need to retreat or get away, I understand. I had to do quite a bit of it myself growing up."

"I don't scare easily."

They kiss. And in that moment, she actually believes there is nothing, *nothing* that can tear them apart.

She's thought a lot of things. She thought it was OK to wear a straw hat in the winter and that the *Friends* spin-off *Joey* would be a big hit. Needless to say, she's been wrong before.

"Darling, you're here!" Tom's mother, the Queen of Snelgravia, shouts, practically skipping out of the house to greet her son, with the family's trusty butler, Mack, trailing behind her. She pulls Tom into a tight hug and kisses him hard on the cheek.

"I'm not letting you leave so easily this time," the Queen tells her son. "And this must be Jenny. How nice to meet you."

The moment of truth. Her one chance to make a good impression on Tom's mom.

Jenny goes in for a hug. The Queen holds out her hand.

Oh no, am I supposed to kiss her hand? She is royal, right? And that's what people do, they kiss the royals' hands.

Jenny grabs the Queen's hand and puts her lips to it. When she pulls away, there's a small lip-shaped red stain on the Queen's hand.

"It's...nice to meet you, dear. You can call me..."

Mom?

"The Queen."

This is going to be a lot harder than I thought, Jenny thinks.

"Mack, take the bags inside, will you? And Jenny?"

"Yes, Queen?" Maybe she is warming up to me after all.

"Why don't you help him out?"

Mack collects the bags while Jenny, desperate to be of use, effortfully picks up her own purse and carries it inside.

When Jenny is safely out of earshot, the queen turns to Tom and looks at him disapprovingly.

"Of all the girls in America, that's who you brought home to Snelgravia?"

"Jenny is incredible. You'll come around. Besides, you wouldn't like any girl I brought home."

"That's not true! What about that Rihanna girl I always hear everyone talking about?"

"Mother, I like Jenny a lot. Besides, I already asked Rihanna out. She said no."

Later that evening, it's the annual Snelgravia state dinner—the most exclusive invitation in the country, yet Jenny would rather be anywhere else. More specifically, she would rather be in her and Tom's apartment, eating Chinese food and watching *The Bleakest Night*, but here she is anyway. And tonight is important. Tonight is the night she shows the Queen that she is worthy of marrying her son. That she is even worthy someday down the line—probably very down the line—of being a leader of their people.

Jenny stares at herself in the jewel-encrusted mirror above her bureau and takes a deep breath. "Not half bad," she says to herself, admiring the deep purple and ivory evening gown, so chosen for Snelgravia's colors by the Queen's staff.

An hour and a half later, Jenny finds herself descending down a grand staircase (seriously grand; this staircase is the size of her whole apartment).

"You can do this. You can do this. You can do this," she keeps telling herself, but she's not quite sure if that's true until she locks eyes with Tom. He's standing at the bottom of the staircase, wearing his Snelgravian finest, and looking, well, like a goddamn prince. He's in the middle of a conversation with some (probably very important) diplomat, but when he looks up and sees Jenny, that doesn't matter anymore. The whole world falls away.

And what does Jenny do in that moment? Well, she falls down the stairs, of course. Face first and everything.

Tom rushes over to help her up. "No one saw," he tells her, lying.

Suddenly, a member of the Royal Court blows a trumpet, indicating that the hundred-some dignitaries and celebrities attending this state dinner (is that the German prime minister talking with Priyanka Chopra and Amal Clooney?) can be seated. A quick scan of the table place cards reveals that the Queen has, in fact, seated Jenny on one side of the table and Tom far, far away at the other end, next to—of course—his ex-girlfriend, Natasha, who looks about as comfortable and at ease in this setting as Jenny feels when she's in a big pair of sweatpants.

"You'll do great. I'll see you after, OK?" Tom says reassuringly, drawing Jenny in for a short kiss.

She takes her seat, sandwiched in between two older dignitaries who smell strongly of scotch and spend the first half-hour of dinner yelling over her in Snelgravian, a language in which so far Jenny only can say "Hello," "How much does this cost?" and "Where is the bathroom?"

But Jenny is behaving herself. Even when she sees Natasha leaning over to whisper flirtatiously in Tom's ear. Even when the Queen winks approvingly in Natasha's direction. Jenny remains steadfast to her commitment to using the appropriate fork for each course.

But as Jenny, or really anyone who has read *The Outsiders* knows, nothing gold can stay.

About an hour into dinner, Jenny feels a tap on her shoulder. She turns to find the Princess of Malgravia, who asks in a breathy voice, "Excuse me? Would you mind trading seats with me for a moment?"

Jenny scans to see where the princess was sitting before and—just her luck—it was right next to Tom and Natasha.

"Of course! Happy to help a girl out," Jenny tells the princess, and makes her way over to Tom and Natasha's corner of the table.

"Hello," she coos, kissing Tom on the cheek.

Before he can reply, the Queen is by their side, demanding to know: "Jenny, what are you doing over here? You were supposed to be sitting *there*," pointing to Jenny's seat. Locked in a heated argument were the princess and the diplomat who had been sitting to Jenny's left.

How could she be so stupid? Table assignments are always made for a reason, she thinks. Who was she to play God?

"We were specifically trying to keep the princess *away* from the Hungarian diplomat." The Queen pauses. "Princess! Please, put that down. That china pre-dates the Ottoman Empire!"

Jenny is crestfallen. How could she be so stupid? Table assignments are always made for a reason, she thinks. Who was she to play God?

BUILD YOUR OWN ROMANTIC COMEDY

Sensing Jenny's obvious moment of weakness, Natasha seizes this as her moment to pounce. She leans in close to Jenny and says:

"I *love* your lipstick. Could you get me one next time you're at CVS?"

 It's time for Jenny to get makeover. Turn to the candles on page 75.

 Jenny is over it. If she punches Natasha in the face, turn to the punch on page 40.

"Hey, isn't that the cute guy you were flirting with last week?" CJ asks Jenny, pointing to a handsome man at the corner of the store, perusing their used books section. CJ's on register duty while Jenny wipes down the counter.

"Oh yeah! That is him."

"Wow, he's even cuter than he was a week ago," CJ says, surveying Tom. "How does he do that?"

"Shh, he's coming over here!" Jenny tells CJ, throwing the cleaning rag at her.

"Hey! Fancy seeing you here," Tom says with a wink, approaching the counter.

"Well, you caught me," Jenny replies, with a laugh.

"She doesn't just work here, she owns the store," CJ, unable to keep quiet, quickly interjects before Jenny can shush her again.

"Wow, this whole place is yours? And at your age too? That's very impressive."

"Well, it was my mom's, and now it's mine," Jenny replies. "But what about you, what do you do?" she asks, hoping to change the subject.

"Me? I'm in real estate. Very boring stuff." He pauses and chews on a thought for a moment. "There's actually something I want to tell you."

"Jenny? What are you doing talking to this guy?" Suddenly, Dave is there, and he's asking Jenny why she's talking to an attractive man. But come to think of it, Dave is always showing up when Jenny is taking to an attractive man.

CJ can't help but intervene. "What do you mean? He's a customer. Jenny owns this store. It's her *job* to talk to customers."

"I *mean* that he's the owner of Thor Capital Equity Liquidators, Inc.!"

The gravity of this proclamation hits Jenny—hard. She doesn't think there's any way that it can be true, but the way Tom is looking at her, with two eyes that should belong to a puppy, she knows it must be.

"Wait, *you're* Tom Thor?"

"Yes, I'm so sorry you had to find out this way. It doesn't change anything I said... or how I feel."

Maybe Tom means it. But it doesn't matter anymore. Nothing does.

"Get out."

If Jenny throws a big party to try to save Toffee, Coffee, and Co., turn to the balloons on page 83.

 CJ is sick of playing second fiddle. If she and Jenny get into a fight, turn to the lemon on page 77.

Chapter Seven

EPHEMERA

Empty pizza boxes litter the conference room. Jenny reclines in a chair, her feet up on the table, where Tom's head is slumped. Their coworkers are similarly exhausted and disengaged.

Tom lifts his head and says, "I can't look at these reports anymore. Get them as far away from me as possible."

Jenny picks up a nearby binder and begins flipping through it. "I think there might be something on page 34."

She squints, eyes exhausted, and, for the first time in what must be years, she takes off her glasses.

Tom looks at Jenny, and when he does it's like he is seeing her—truly seeing her—for the first time.

"Oh no, did I get cheese stuck in my teeth? That happens sometimes," Jenny says, surreptitiously rubbing a finger over her front teeth.

"No, it's just...you look so different without glasses," Tom replies, taken aback.

Suddenly, all of their coworkers are similarly transfixed, looking at Jenny like she's Lady Gaga doing a drop-in at an open mic.

"I look literally the same whether or not I have my glasses on," Jenny says, perplexed.

"Haha! That's funny. You're funny," one of her (male) coworkers says, adding a loud chortle at the end.

"...It wasn't a joke."

Suddenly, Cynthia bursts into the room.

"Remember, I want proposals by 5 p.m. tomorrow, people," she announces, barely looking up from her cell phone. Her eyes gaze around the room and eventually land on Jenny.

"Who's the new girl?" she asks, with something other than vague disdain.

"It's me," Jenny replies. "I've worked here for five years. I took my glasses off and—"

"Break them. I never want to see them on your face again."

If Jenny and Tom have to stay late to work on a project together, turn to the easel on page 46.

 If Jenny and Tom have no choice but to go on a work-related road trip together, turn to the car on page 49.

 If Jenny and Tom start spending more time together as friends, turn to the bicycle on page 79.

"I can't believe I let you talk me into this" Jenny says to CJ, in between huffing and puffing from her stationary spin bike.

"A 7 a.m. spin-yoga class? What's not to like?" CJ replies, peppily.

"OK! Off your bikes! Get in downward dog," the class instructor announces, jumping off her bike and assuming the yoga pose. The class quickly follows suit, with Jenny half a beat behind.

"So, you like him then?" CJ asks, referring to the not bad, OK, very good, OK, downright incredible kiss Jenny recently shared with Tom.

"High kick, everybody!" the instructor calls out.

"No! I hate him!" Jenny says, firing off a kick.

"Back on the bike, everybody!" Another call from the instructor.

"But you can't stop talking about him. *And* you kissed," CJ replies.

"So? Do you like everyone you kiss?" Jenny has her there.

"Fair point," CJ concedes.

"Shhh!" a rider behind them calls out. Jenny and CJ chat on, ignoring her completely.

"This class is so hard. I don't know how I let you talk me into this every time," Jenny says, painstakingly pedaling away.

The rider behind them desperately wants to exercise away her anxieties about the three new social media accounts she just landed.

"Maybe it would be easier if you two stopped talking," the annoyed rider calls out from behind them. Even still, they ignore her.

"So, you're attracted to him?" CJ prods.

"I mean, yes, he's objectively good-looking," Jenny answers.

"And he makes you laugh?"

"Well, yes, but only because he's such a big dumb idiot."

"Instructor! Instructor! Will you please tell these women to be quiet?" The rider behind them desperately wants to exercise away her anxieties about the three new social media accounts she just landed—without having to listen to some woman complain about a man, of all things.

"Wow, narc much?" CJ asks, turning around. Everyone in the class has stopped pedaling in order to watch whether these three women are going to fight, because at the very least, it'll give them something to talk about at brunch.

The instructor turns off the music. She relaxes from her pedaling position on the bike and looks squarely at Jenny and CJ.

"You," she says, zeroing in on Jenny. "You obviously like whatever guy you're talking about, so just get over yourself and go out with him. And please leave my class immediately."

 If Jenny gets an amazing job offer, turn to the suitcase on page 92.

 To see things from CJ's perspective, turn to the plate on page 39.

 CJ is sick of how absent Jenny has been lately. If she and Jenny get into a fight, turn to the lemon on page 77.

BUILD YOUR OWN ROMANTIC COMEDY

Jenny sits patiently in the waiting room for over an hour, her hands crossed over her lap. She's about to throw in the towel and go home when Mauricio, an impeccably dressed bald man in his fifties, breezes into the room, flanked by a group of European women, each of them more stunning than the last.

"Bonjour, Mademoiselle Jennifer," Mauricio begins, grabbing Jenny by the hand, pulling her up to stand, and distributing a kiss on each of her cheeks.

"Oh, please, call me Jenny," she replies, brushing off his formalities.

"I absolutely will not!" he chides. He glares at her and his female minions follow suit.

How did I screw this up already? Jenny wonders.

Before she can say anything, Mauricio starts laughing, and in time the female minions follow suit. Confused, Jenny joins in too.

"So, I don't really need anything too crazy. I know I'm supposed to be here for a makeover, but I just think a nice haircut will suffice. Maybe some bangs?"

At this, Mauricio recommences laughing.

"That is a good one. You will get the full treatment. That is what I am being paid for. That is what Mauricio does." He pauses, then leans in close. "But no bangs. After I gave Zooey Deschanel hers, I said, 'Never again,' for a master knows when his work is done."

Jenny considers this for a second. He has a point.

First comes the manicure. Then the pedicure. Then the facial. Then the deep tissue massage, followed by a hair color and cut.

Champagne in hand, Jenny thinks to herself, I could get used to this.

That is...until the waxing. So much waxing. More waxing than Jenny thought a body could withstand or was necessary even. Jenny wonders about her role in the patriarchy, and her willingness to go along with this makeover at all signals her compliance with it. And then she thinks, that is a bigger question to explore, perhaps another time.

> "But no bangs. After I gave Zooey Deschanel hers, I said, 'Never again,' for a master knows when his work is done."

And that, of course, is quickly followed by a full shopping spree, during which time Jenny tries on outfits she could never imagine having use for: a hot pink poncho, multiple (very impractical) ball gowns, a powder blue tuxedo, a bikini with not nearly the amount of coverage she demands from her swimsuits, and a sweater she *thinks* has real dog fur on it. All of this while Mauricio, ever the good sport, plays Cyndi Lauper's "Girls Just Wanna Have Fun." The music blasts from a set of speakers held by one of Mauricio's minions, likely the head minion for such an important task to be delegated to her.

Jenny has to admit though, at the end of the full seven days, with her new hair and her new clothes and her completely exfoliated body, she looks *good*. Mauricio thinks so too. He is crying.

"Even more beautiful than Zooey Deschanel's bangs."

 If the Queen wants to have a word with Jenny. Turn to the crown on page 98.

 Oh no, while Jenny was getting a makeover, something bad could be brewing in Snelgravia. Turn to the scales on page 41 to find out.

BUILD YOUR OWN ROMANTIC COMEDY

Jenny works her way through throngs of young, pretty people, only to come upon yet another throng of young, pretty people. But Jenny is still at a loss to find the young, pretty person she was looking for—CJ, to be specific.

"Hey, what is this line for?" A guy calls out, snapping a picture of the two-hundred-person line, after which he will most certainly post the picture to his Instagram story with the question, "Can you believe this line?"

"It's this new tapioca pudding place. And you can choose what flavors you want the lumps to be!" one woman in line replies.

> "I played so much Candy Crush all morning and now everywhere I look I just see little pieces of fruit.

Jenny promised she'd meet CJ hours ago, the latest promise in a series of promises she has not kept lately.

She pushes her way to the front of the crowd. Finally, Jenny sees her. She slips her arm through CJ's. "I'm so sorry I'm late, but your tapioca is on me—all the lumps you want."

One problem: The woman's arm she's holding? Not CJ's, but in fact, a stranger's. A stranger who, while she does resemble CJ, is a completely different human entirely and one who does not enjoy being grabbed by Jenny, no matter how charming Jenny is known to be.

"Uh, hello? I think it's me you owe that tapioca pudding to," Jenny hears from behind her. She turns to find the actual CJ standing nearby.

CJ pulls Jenny into the line with her. "Where have you been?" she asks. "I've been waiting for you for literally hours. I played so much Candy Crush all morning and now everywhere I look I just see little pieces of fruit. That guy's face? Lemon drop. That lady over there? Peppermint. And you? A blue globe thing."

"I'm so sorry. I got caught up—"

"You're *always* getting caught up these days. Like, where have you been?"

"You know I have a lot going on right now," Jenny begins.

"Excuse me, are you cutting the line? Because you can't cut the line," a Very Annoying Person who probably does not have very many friends insists from behind them.

"You're not the only one who has stuff going on!" CJ tells Jenny, her voice rising in volume.

"I know that," Jenny counters, staring down at the sidewalk below her.

"Well, it'd be great if you started acting like it," CJ replies.

"One of you has to get off the line, it's only fair," the Very Annoying Person interjects again.

"We've had this planned for months and you couldn't even bother to show up on time. And *you know* how much I love tapioca pudding," CJ says.

The Very Annoying Person chimes in again: "I'm waiting!"

"She can stay. I'll leave," CJ says. "She always gets the pudding." And with that, CJ walks away, leaving Jenny sad, alone, and that much closer to artisanal tapioca pudding.

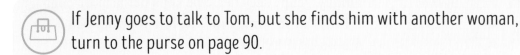 If Jenny goes to talk to Tom, but she finds him with another woman, turn to the purse on page 90.

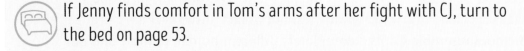 If Jenny finds comfort in Tom's arms after her fight with CJ, turn to the bed on page 53.

Over the next few weeks, without any kind of formal decision-making or active choice, Tom becomes a consistent presence in Jenny's life.

Re-watching *Friends* on her couch? Check.

Bike-riding on beautiful days in the park? Check.

Laughing at each other's terrible attempts to do an Australian accent? Check.

Taking Tom as her plus-one to CJ's annual Fourth of July blowout bash? Check.

Going to midnight arthouse movies and then the diner after, where they steal each other's fries and dissect whatever it is they just saw? Check.

Re-watching *Friends* again on the couch? Check again.

Falling asleep on Tom's shoulder? Also check.

Jenny wakes with a start to find she and Tom have made their way to season seven of *Friends*. The last thing she remembers is her and Tom being unable to come to a clear conclusion as to whether or not Ross and Rachel were on a break. Her head is on his shoulder, his head on the couch's arm.

"No, Marcel!" Tom mutters in his sleep, but aside from that outburst, he sleeps peacefully. Jenny considers waking him but thinks better of it. He can stay here. It's just the couch. Who cares? She directs that last question toward the voice of CJ in her head, who is saying, "Yeah, right, it's just the couch." What's next? The shower?

Jenny grabs a blanket from the foot of the couch and throws it over Tom, retreating to her bedroom and leaving Tom alone with his dreams about Marcel, the monkey from *Friends*.

To see Jenny and Tom embrace their musical side, turn to the music note on page 89.

 If Jenny catches Tom with Natasha, turn to the purse on page 90.

 If Jenny is excited about the wrong guy but can't see it, turn to the bar sign on page 62.

BUILD YOUR OWN ROMANTIC COMEDY

It's late, and Jenny is starving. She can't deny that she's a little drunk too. And based on the fact that he is currently ranting about the genius of *The Departed*, Jenny has to assume that Tom is too.

"Enough, I get it! It's a metaphor! It's all a metaphor!" she says, cutting him off. "Now can we *please* get something to eat. It's going to start raining any second."

They're aimlessly walking down what just so happened to be empty streets. They're sticking to the sidewalks, but it's the kind of night where it wouldn't matter if they didn't.

"It's a perfect summer night. No way is it going to rain."

He is right about that. It is a beautiful evening. But Jenny has a knack for sensing the calm before the storm.

"Ooh, you know, we're actually one block from this taco stand I loooove."

"Well, there's a Halal cart *I* love and it's also only one block away."

"Trust me, you're going to want to try these tacos." Jenny holds her ground.

"*You're* going to want to try this chicken and rice." Huh, so is Tom.

"OK, I have an idea: You go get your Halal, I'll get my tacos, and we'll meet back here in 30," Jenny proposes.

A half-hour later, Jenny and Tom sit on the front steps of an empty-for-the-night office building, the silence of a sleeping city almost deafening.

She takes a bite of Tom's Halal, and him, her tacos.

"Mmm," Tom says, "I guess we were both right."

"Well, me more so than you."

"Why do you say that?" he asks.

She points to the sky. "It's raining."

Suddenly, without warning, and with no regard to the fact that the rain is really starting to come down, Tom's mouth is on hers. They're kissing, and Jenny can't even remember who was right or wrong in the first place.

To see Jenny and Tom embrace their musical side, turn to the music note on page 89.

 If Jenny and Tom spend the night together, turn to the bed on page 53.

"Oh my god, I haven't seen this many smart people in one room since we went to that Emily Nussbaum talkback," CJ says, marveling at the success of their fundraiser to save Toffee, Coffee, and Co. "And I haven't seen this many good-looking people in one room since we crashed that dinner party at Greta Gerwig's."

CJ has a point; all of the city's literati and then some have come out to help them raise enough money to keep Toffee, Coffee, and Co. in business. The store is packed to the gills with people, and their laughter and good cheer fill the air with hope. There are signed books from Haruki Murakami, Zadie Smith, and Robert Caro; toffee-making classes with one of the city's top toffee chefs; and a lifetime supply of coffee beans, all up for auction. There are cheese plates as far as the eye could see. And white wine. Lots of it.

As CJ sidles away to help pass out more drinks, Jenny stops, taking it all in. This is the culmination of years of her mother's—and then her own—work to make Toffee, Coffee, and Co., a neighborhood staple. She hates to think that it all might be gone soon.

Hours later, after CJ and Dave have helped clean up, Jenny lingers in the store, not quite ready for the night to be over. When she hears the door opening and its bell chime, she calls out, "Sorry, we're closed!"

"Am I late?"

Tom. Of course. Like an ant coming to pick over leftover crumbs. A hot ant, perhaps, but that's beside the point.

"The party's over."

"It doesn't have to be," Tom remarks. Cocking his head to the side, he pulls out a bottle of whiskey from his inner coat pocket. "What's one drink with the enemy?"

Now, Jenny is intrigued.

"Ah, a drink with the enemy. How the Romans did it," Jenny replies. In actuality, she has no idea how the Romans did it, one way or another, but something about it sounded right.

Tom grabs two empty glasses leftover from the party and pours a whiskey neat for them each.

"You know, I don't want your store to close. It's all my dad. He's the head of the company. I'm just his errand boy," Tom says.

"Ah, a rich guy with daddy issues. How original."

"I know, I know. But believe me, I don't like it any more than you do."

"I find that a little hard to believe."

Tom pauses for a moment and pulls a small, folded-up piece of paper out of his pocket. He hands it to Jenny and says, "Maybe this will convince you."

He downs the last of his whiskey and heads to the door. Before he leaves, he gives Jenny one last look. It seems like he's on the verge of saying something—something big, something important—but instead he shakes his head and walks out the door.

She unfolds the piece of paper to find that it's a check. But it's not just any check: a check for the exact amount needed for Toffee, Coffee, and Co. to pay its rent at the new, increased price for five whole years.

 If Jenny embraces her outdoorsy side, turn to the mountains on page 44.

 To see Jenny and Tom begin spending time together, turn to the bicycle on page 79.

 The fundraiser doesn't help. If Toffee, Coffee, and Co. is closing down, turn to the box on page 96.

BUILD YOUR OWN ROMANTIC COMEDY

Jenny remembers it as if it were yesterday: Bad orthodontia and cans of Pabst Blue Ribbon as far as the eye can see. An unfinished basement with wood paneling, brimming with teenagers. Jenny's *first* high school cool kids party—and maybe her only one, if she didn't prove herself worthy.

She took a sip of the warm PBR, scanning the room desperately for a friendly face. Suddenly, she saw her lifelong best friend, Tom, cutting a path through the masses.

"Is this what everyone else has been doing while we were at Mock Trial?" Tom asked. Jenny tried to hand him her beer, but he shook her off.

"No, I need to keep my wits about me to navigate a social ecosystem so complex."

Jenny laughed. Tom was funny! Had he always been this funny?

Before Jenny could answer her own question, their high school's self-anointed Queen Bee, Natasha, was in front of her, demanding her attention.

"Are you two, like, ever not glued at the hip?"

"Actually, Natasha, we're glued at the foot, thank you very much," Tom retorted. Jenny snorted and giggled, and Natasha rolled her eyes.

"Well, we're all playing spin the bottle—if you care to join us." Natasha leaned in conspiratorially and said, "And Jenny, I heard Dave is hoping the bottle lands on *you*." Immediately, a million thoughts stormed through Jenny's mind, chief among them: Did Dave really say that? Did that mean he wants to kiss her? How did Natasha know she liked him? But they always knew. Somehow, they always knew.

Seated cross-legged in a circle, half a dozen teenage boys and girls took turns spinning an empty Smirnoff Ice bottle. Finally, it was Dave's turn. The bottle made five achingly, dizzyingly slow revolutions. Jenny held her breath. Finally, *finally*, the bottle landed square between Jenny and some girl from her AP Econ class—Deborah?

"I'll pass," Deborah said, scornfully.

Dave pretended to be hurt, offended. "Well, is *not* Jenny an option?" he asked.

Immediately, Jenny felt her cheeks burning up as the group surrounding her began to laugh, slow at first, and then all at once in a cacophony. She ran out of the room, but not before she saw Natasha smirking in her direction.

Tom followed Jenny to her car and found her sitting in its passenger seat. He climbed inside.

"I'll drive you home," Tom volunteered. Jenny was drunk.

"God, so embarrassing. I can't wait to get out of here. This stupid town. These stupid people. I hate all of them." She looked at Tom, as if seeing him—really *seeing* him—for the first time. "Except you."

"Well, you know, I don't hate you either," Tom said, putting his arm around Jenny like he had a million times before. But that night, it felt different.

Jenny turned her face around and kissed Tom. He met her there, but only momentarily.

"I don't want to be your second choice." He turned the key in the ignition and drove her home like he had so many times before, but everything would be different after that. She'd broken something between them.

 If Jenny catches Tom with Natasha in present day, turn to the purse on page 90.

 If Jenny needs her mom—and her advice—turn to the pillow on page 111.

BUILD YOUR OWN ROMANTIC COMEDY

Tom stands in position. Focus up, gaze steady. The moment of truth.

The baseball pitching machine chucks out a high fast one. He swings—and *crack*—his bat makes contact with the ball, just like it has hundreds, perhaps even thousands, of times before.

"Heyoooo!" Tom's two best friends and constant batting cage companions, Steve and Mark, call out from behind him. They high five. A lot.

The baseball soars through the sky and above the field ahead. Tom throws his hands in the air victoriously.

"Heyoooo!" Tom's two best friends and constant batting cage companions, Steve and Mark, call out from behind him. They high five. A lot. Steve is wearing a band t-shirt underneath his blazer and is a vegetarian, whereas Mark wears ties all the time, even to the batting cages, and only eats steak. The three men have nothing in common, and yet, they are best friends.

"You are on *fire* tonight," Steve says. "What's got you in such a good mood?"

Tom says nothing, but grins as wide as a Cheshire cat.

"Ooh, it's a girl, isn't it?" Mark theorizes.

Steve agrees. "Oh yeah, it's gotta be a girl. What's her name?"

"Hey! You know I don't kiss and tell!" Tom says mischievously, toweling off.

"Please. Since when?" Steve asks. He does have a point; previously Tom would kiss and tell anyone who would listen.

"Since..." Tom has to think about it. Steve does have a point. "Well, since I really like this girl."

If Jenny goes to see Tom but finds him with Natasha, turn to the purse on page 90.

 If Jenny and Tom spend the night together, turn to the bed on page 53.

BUILD YOUR OWN ROMANTIC COMEDY

"Ooh, I love a good, old-fashioned jukebox," Jenny exclaims, making her way over to the jukebox in the corner of the bar. Tom follows.

"You *have* to pick something good. You're basically bar DJ when you put a song on the jukebox. That's a lot of responsibility," he warns.

"I'm not going to pick a *bad* song."

"No one thinks they're picking a bad song...and yet, so often they do."

Jenny flips through the options, eventually settling on "Rocket Man" by Elton John.

"'Rocket Man'?!" Tom asks, incredulous. "Please. So overrated."

"Hey, the people here seem to like it." Jenny gestures toward the rest of the bar patrons, who have started bopping their heads and tapping their toes accordingly.

Maybe it's the three tequila sodas Tom had ordered them, or maybe Jenny is feeling particularly good tonight, but she starts singing along—loudly. The thing is, though, the rest of the bar joins in, until finally, Tom has to recognize that he's the wrong one.

She climbs up onto the bar. She doesn't know who she thinks she is tonight—maybe it's the cowboy boots she decided to slip on that are emboldening her—but dancing on bars is not typical Jenny fashion.

"OK, maybe this song isn't *so* bad," Tom concedes. Jenny pulls him by the hand and up onto the bar, where they both start dancing, the rest of the bar cheering them on.

It occurs to her: This is the most fun she's had since...well, since ever, maybe.

 Jenny *needs* to talk to CJ about this. Turn to the stationary bike on page 73.

 If Jenny and Tom spend the night together, turn to the bed on page 53.

It's one week later—a lifetime, in Jenny's world. Jenny has been waiting for Tom for over a half an hour when she makes a decision that will change the course of both of their lives forever.

When Tom is late to meet her and he doesn't return one of her "Where are you?" and "Is everything OK?" texts, she thinks, I'll pop over to his apartment to make sure nothing is wrong.

Jenny is across the street from Tom's when she looks up and sees a man and woman kissing outside of his building. Huh, she thinks. I didn't know there was a couple living in Tom's complex. They must be new.

That is until the couple breaks apart from their kiss and it isn't a couple new to the building at all. To Jenny's horror, it's Tom and a woman whose face Jenny couldn't quite make out, but could only be...Natasha.

Jenny doesn't know whether she's surprised or if this felt truly inevitable all along. Does it even matter?

She lets go of her purse and it falls to the ground with a loud *thud*—so loud, in fact, that the sound manages to attract both Tom's and Natasha's attention. Tom looks horrified; Natasha, smug, or so Jenny imagines, as she can't bring herself to look at her face.

So much for retreating to my bedroom for eternity peacefully, Jenny thinks, as she reaches down to scoop up everything that's fallen out of her purse and onto the sidewalk: tampons, lipstick, miscellaneous coins, tissues—you name it, it's splayed out on the ground in front of her.

Tom crosses the street and quickly picks up Jenny's bag before she can.

"I don't need your help," she tells him, crouched down on the ground, picking up her ephemeral items.

"It's not what it looks like, Jenny, I promise."

"It never is," she tells him, grabbing her purse and beginning to walk away.

"Please, can we talk about this?" Tom pleads. And deep, deep down, Jenny wants to talk to him, wants to forget it never happened, wants to let him push her hair behind her ear and kiss her. But she knows that she can't and she won't. So instead she says:

BUILD YOUR OWN ROMANTIC COMEDY

"I don't think there's anything left to say." And then she leaves.

 If Jenny can't deal and runs away, turn to the airplane on page 118.

 If Jenny becomes so obsessed with work she forgets about Tom, turn to the hourglass on page 36.

 If Jenny wanders the streets, sad, turn to the traffic light on page 109.

Climbing up the stairs to Jenny's apartment, Tom rehearses over and over again the speech he plans to recite once he arrives. About his feelings and how they've changed. Because sometimes, whether you like it or not— even if you really don't like it— how you look at somebody can suddenly shift. One day they're your friend and you suddenly can't live without them. Or even if you could, it doesn't mean you want to.

Tom knocks on the door, ready for the moment of truth.

"Hey, are you ready to go..." to dinner, he's about to ask, when she opens the door and lets him in. That is, until he realizes that Jenny has multiple suitcases open, scattered across her apartment, and everything from blazers to bathing suits strewn over her furniture.

"On vacation, apparently?"

"Oh my god, we were supposed to go to dinner! I'm so sorry. I completely spaced," Jenny replies, absentmindedly picking up a stack of books and throwing them into an open suitcase.

"Forget about dinner. I have something I need to tell you," Tom begins. "Although it looks like you might have something to tell me too."

"So months and months ago I applied for this job in Nashville, never expecting that I would get it and I completely forgot about it until they called me up out of nowhere and offered it to me," Jenny tells him excitedly. "Can you believe that?"

He can't.

Just tell her how you feel and maybe she'll stay, he thinks. But before he can, Jenny says, "I know, I know, it's so unlike me to do anything spontaneous like this. But it's such a good opportunity, and I've always wanted to live in Nashville. The food, the music..."

She continues like that for a while. Seeing how excited Jenny is about her new opportunity, Tom can't bring himself to tell her how he feels. If she decides to go anyway, he'll be devastated. And if she turns the job down and stays for him, well, she might eventually come to resent him for it. A lose-lose situation.

"And obviously I am going to get a pair of cowboy boots," Jenny says. Then, emerging from her reverie, she asks, "Wait, did you have something you wanted to say?"

"Yes, in fact. I have something *very* important I want to ask you," he proceeds. Jenny holds her breath. What on earth?

"Can I help you pack?"

 To see Tom chase Jenny at the airport, turn to the airplane on page 118.

 If Jenny becomes so obsessed with work she forgets about Tom, turn to the hourglass on page 36.

Everyone, no matter who you ask, has their spot. The spot they go to when they don't know what to do or where to turn. A place that makes them feel at peace when the world is in upheaval.

For Jenny, her spot has always been Chambers Pond, where her mother took her when she was a little girl and where she continues to return now, as a woman.

Tom knows that when Jenny isn't picking up her phone, answering his texts, or firing off tweets about how much she loves the *Great British Baking Show* that this is where he can find her.

She sits on a bench in front of the pond, watching the ducks swim by.

When Tom finds her, it's impossible for him to know how long she'd been sitting there—minutes, hours—if you told him weeks, he would believe it.

He sits next to Jenny, fully prepared to launch into the whole spiel: How much he cares about her, why they're perfect together, that *he's* the guy she should be with and it's been obvious ever since the moment they met, even if he couldn't quite see it then. That, yes, they don't see eye-to-eye on everything (or anything, really), but that's the best way for each of them to learn and grow.

Before he can start, though, Jenny said, quietly: "I've been coming here ever since I was a kid."

"I know."

"And for the longest time I wondered, 'This is such a small pond, why wouldn't they try to make it bigger, better? But some things should remain the way they are. Sometimes if you try to build on something, or improve it, you end up ruining what was already perfect the way it was."

What is she talking about? Tom is completely prepared to ask for clarity, when suddenly, regretfully, he completely understands what Jenny is trying to tell him. It's not really about the pond, it's about their relationship.

"You're staying with Dave, aren't you?"

She gives him a small, mournful smile and squeezes his hand, slowly nodding her head. Together, they watch the ducks in silence, until, finally, there were none left on the water.

If Tom is with Natasha now, turn to the dog on page 106.

 If Jenny marries Dave, turn to the hearts on page 126.

 Is Jenny questioning her decision to be with Dave? Turn to the TV on page 108.

Jenny inhales, deeply breathing in that unique combination of smells Toffee, Coffee and Co., has to offer: old books, sweet, sticky toffee, and rich coffee beans. She can't believe that she won't get to wake up every day and smell that smell, greet her favorite customers, and work alongside her two best friends.

But nothing lasts forever—especially not cute small, local businesses. Something has to come next. She just doesn't know what yet. Jenny had agonized over whether or not to take Tom's money. But at the end of the day, she doesn't want to owe him anything. This is what she has to do.

"CJ, will you hand me the packing tape?" Jenny asks her best friend, as she packs up yet another box, one of many surrounding them throughout the store. CJ stares out the window, unresponsive.

"CJ?"

"Sorry, but I don't want to pack! It's not fair that we have to leave."

"I don't like it either, but we don't have a choice. We can't make that kind of rent, even after the increased sales from the press we got and that party we threw. It's just not sustainable."

Desperate, CJ asks, "But if I worked for free?"

Jenny gets up from her spot on the floor, walks over to CJ, and with her hand on her shoulder says, "You basically already do."

They laugh. Finally, CJ says, "Yeah, I know. I have three other jobs."

After all the boxes are packed up, and Jenny and CJ have forced Dave to haul them to Jenny's apartment, the two women find themselves in the completely empty store.

"Wow," CJ says, trailing her finger along one of the empty bookshelves. "Not a speck of dust."

"Of course not! My mother taught me better than that," Jenny says, her voice cracking slightly at the end.

CJ throws her arm around Jenny's shoulders. "She'd be really proud of you, you know that, right?"

"I just can't help but think that I'm letting her down."

CJ shakes her head. "Never." Jenny can only hope that CJ is right.

And with that, the two women walk out the store for the last time, closing the light and the door behind them.

 If Jenny wanders the streets, devastated, lost, and thinking about Tom, turn to the traffic light on page 109.

 If Jenny thinks about moving back home, turn to the house on page 20.

 Is there a magical solution that can save Toffee, Coffee, and Co.? Turn to the package on page 113 to find out.

What does one do in Snelgravia on a Saturday afternoon? Well, if you're royalty—or at the very least, a member of the upper echelon—the answer to that question is play polo, of course. And that's exactly where you can find Tom, which means that's exactly where you can find Jenny, sitting on a nearby bench, watching him and his comrades play.

"He's good, isn't he?" the Queen asks, taking a seat on the bench beside Jenny. Jenny is surprised for a number of reasons. First, because she didn't know royalty sat on benches, and second, because she and the Queen had never spent any time alone before.

"He's very talented," Jenny replies, wondering where all of this is leading.

"He'll be king one day, you know," the Queen says, and suddenly Jenny has a very clear picture of where this is heading.

"I know."

"He'll have responsibilities that most people can only dream of."

"I know that too."

"And he'll need a...particular kind of wife."

Jenny steels herself, getting ready to give the speech she's had prepared in her head for days now.

"I know you don't like me, you haven't since the moment we met. But Tom and I love each other. I want to spend my life with him. I know what I would be sacrificing."

"Do you?" the Queen pauses. "Because I thought I did."

OK, now Jenny is confused. "I thought..."

"That I was born queen? No, no. While my family was from a noble line of Snelgravians, it was Tom's father to whom the crown truly belonged. And I loved him, I still do, but if I had known then what I know now, I might have chosen differently. That's all I am asking you to do: Really think about your life if you choose this. No privacy, the inability to make your own choices. If you and Tom want to get married, you have my blessing—"

Jenny tries to interrupt, but before she can, the Queen continues.

"But make sure you're ready to have this life, because when Snelgravians say 'forever' in our vows, we mean it."

With this, the Queen, in all her regal glory, stands and walks away. Jenny gazes out to the pitch, where Tom has just scored a goal. His teammates gather around him, cheering him on and patting him on the back. For the first time since she met Tom, she questions whether she wants to spend the rest of her life with him.

 If you think Tom has been paying too much attention to his love life and not to the current affairs of Snelgravia, turn to the scales on page 41.

 If Jenny catches Tom with Natasha, turn to the purse on page 90.

Jenny knew her time using an assumed identity couldn't last forever. The new family, the wonderful boyfriend, all of that money, and with it the chance to make a difference, but she didn't expect it to end this way.

It's like an out-of-body experience. There's ringing in her ears and everyone feels so far away, and yet she can still make out Natasha saying the words "I told you she's not who she said she is," and the incredibly disappointed hurt and betrayed look on Tom's face.

Jenny and Tom were having a normal day (hanging out in her library, reading books, sometimes kissing between page-flipping)—or what had become normal for Jenny, at least—when Natasha came bursting into the library with Cecilia trailing along after her.

"Natasha, I can't understand what could be so important that called me in the middle of a facial to get in my car from my estate and drive over to *this* estate," Cecilia says, flipping her Chanel sunglasses onto her forehead, "Oh, hello, Jenny, Tom, good to see you," the typically muted greeting you might expect from a woman of Cecilia's stature to give her son and his girlfriend.

"You'll see in just a second," Natasha replies in a sinister tone, and Jenny knows this cannot be good.

"Jennie," Natasha calls out to the hallway. "You can come in now."

"What are you talking about? Jenny is right here," Tom says, coming to her defense. "And you've had it out for her since day one."

"You'll see why in a *just* a second," Natasha replies, impatiently. "Jennie! Will you get in here?"

And suddenly, Jenny's doppelgänger enters, looking every bit like Jenny...except dirtier. Everyone looks confused, except Natasha, who continues to look as smug as Cinderella's stepsister moments after she leaves Cinderella behind and hightails it for the ball.

"How...?" Tom asked, pointing back and forth between Jenny and Jennie.

"I'll tell you how. This Jennie—Jennie with an *ie*—never left the ashram! She's been there this whole time."

"So...who is this?" Cecilia asks, pointing at Jenny.

BUILD YOUR OWN ROMANTIC COMEDY

"Some rando, whom all of you were willing to open your lives—and *more* —to," Natasha says, throwing Tom an incriminating look.

"Jenny?" he asks.

"Yes?" Jenny and Jennie reply in tandem.

"I mean, 'Jenny with a y' Jenny. Is this true? Have you been lying about who you are and how you spell your name?"

"No. I mean, yes, I'm not the Jennie you thought I was. But everything else about me is true! I swear."

> "This whole time I thought you were someone else. Someone who spelled their name J-e-n-n-i-e. And now none of that is true."

"How am I supposed to ever believe another word you say? This whole time I thought you were someone else. Someone who spelled their name J-e-n-n-i-e. And now none of that is true. I can't be here right now." And with that, Tom storms out.

"Well, what about you? Don't you have anything to say for yourself?" Cecilia asks Jennie, who, in response, takes out a pen and a pad of paper. She scribbles furiously, and then hands the pad to Cecilia.

Cecilia reads: "I have taken a decade-long vow of silence and was brought here under duress by Natasha, whom I see has gone up a size since I left. I would like to return to the ashram immediately, as I believe ridding myself of my worldly possessions is the only way I can remain good and pure. Also, Cecilia, your Botox looks great." Cecilia paused, considering this. "Thank you."

Jenny suddenly feels desperate—to make herself understood, to go back in time and fix all of this, to be miles and miles away from here and all of these people. But instead all that comes out is, "I have to find Tom."

To see Tom confront Jenny about her behavior, turn to the speech bubble on page 105.

If Jenny runs away, turn to the airplane on page 118.

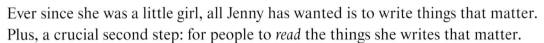

Ever since she was a little girl, all Jenny has wanted is to write things that matter. Plus, a crucial second step: for people to *read* the things she writes that matter.

And with her new article about members of Tom's—or rather, the mayor's, as Jenny should get used to calling him again—administration getting in bed with big-money developers, she has achieved that in one fell swoop. She was the toast of the newsroom that morning, and she's already received a number of congratulatory emails and notable retweets.

There is only one person Jenny thinks might not be so thrilled with her, and that person is Tom, who…is actually storming into the newsroom right now, holding the newspaper in his hand.

"What the hell is this?" he demands.

"Mr. Mayor, to what do we owe the pleasure?" Cynthia coos, dunking a teabag into her hot water-filled NPR mug.

"So you lied to me? This whole time, you lied to me?"

"I was undercover," Jenny explains. "It wasn't personal."

"You used me!"

"Tom, I'm sorry, I had to go undercover to learn more about your deputy mayor and his dirty deal with the developers. That's how this works."

"Yeah, I guess I just thought you were different."

The whole newsroom is silent, watching as Jenny and Tom trade barbs.

Tom begins to walk out the door, but not before turning around and telling Jenny, "For the record, you were a terrible assistant."

"Certainly seems like there's more to *that* story," Cynthia remarks.

You have no idea, Jenny muses.

She knows she did the right thing. It was a good story. She had to report it. She just wishes she could have done it without hurting him.

If Jenny wanders the streets, sad and lost, turn to the traffic light on page 109.

 If Jenny gets fired for being an unprofessional journalist, turn to the file folder on page 42.

Chapter Eight

EVERYONE IS SAD

Jenny stares at Tom. He stares back. He hasn't spoken in what feels like a very long time. Too long. He's not only quiet, but completely still. The kind of still where you think you might need to call a hospital because the person in front of you has entered a fugue state or call the police because the person in front of you looks like they might kill someone.

"Tom, say something, anything, please," Jenny says. She's getting hungry, and if they're going to just sit here like this in his kitchen, they might as well order food or something.

"So this whole time...this *whole time*...you've been lying to me?" he asks.

"Not the *whole* time," Jenny replies. Tom looks at her like, What, do you think I was born yesterday?

"OK, yes, I guess the whole time," she concedes.

"So every conversation we had was founded on a lie?"

Jenny is about to protest, but before she can, he continues.

"Every inside joke?"

Before Jenny can object, there's more —

"Every kiss?"

She's got the hang of it by now.

"Every time," his voice drops to a whisper, "every time...we made love?"

Waiting for more, Jenny remains silent.

"Well?" he prompts.

"Tom, it wasn't like that. I care about you so, *so* much," Jenny begs. Some might even call it pleading.

"How am I supposed to believe a word you say?"

And for once, she doesn't have an answer.

 If Jenny wanders around, sad, turn to the traffic light on page 109.

 If Jenny finally confronts Natasha, turn to the punch on page 40.

Tom is back together with his ex-girlfriend Natasha, and things are going well. Or at least, he wants them to be. He goes to brunch with her. He opens doors for her. He asks questions about her day, good or bad. He is every bit the supportive, caring boyfriend.

At least, on paper.

Because, of course, there is still the Jenny of it all.

Try as Tom might to push Jenny from the margins of his mind, he constantly finds her creeping back in. He checks his email, hoping to see she's reached out, or finds himself beginning text messages to her with a picture of a cute dog he'd seen that day. More than once, Natasha has asked him a question, only for her to have to repeat herself because he was too busy staring into space, reminiscing on his time with Jenny.

But Jenny is in the past now. Natasha is his future, it seems. He just can't quite picture it.

 If Jenny can't bear to let Tom get married without a fight, turn to the pump on page 115.

 If Jenny wanders the city, sad, turn to the traffic light on page 109.

When Jenny arrives at the office, Tom is in her face immediately, apologizing and telling her what a huge mistake he's made. Save it, she tells him. She's spent hours upon hours prepping for this very moment. If she can't sell Cynthia and whoever it is that tells Cynthia what to do to save *Woman*, the magazine will fold, and she'll have to say goodbye to the job that's been more of a home to her than anywhere else.

"I remember when I was a little girl," Jenny begins, standing in the front of *Woman* magazine's gigantic, 88th-floor conference room, "and all I wanted was to be old enough to read *Woman*. *Woman* taught me everything I needed to know. How to be strong"—she glances over at Tom for this part—"How to be independent. How to pick out the right lipstick. She takes a deep breath and runs her hands against her miraculously crease-free charcoal gray pencil skirt.

"But times are different today. Different than when *Woman* was founded in the 1960s, and different even than when I was a little girl. We don't need to appeal to men. We never have. We need to make *Woman* a more inclusive magazine—or it will be the end of us."

She looks directly at Cynthia, waiting for her approval to go on. Cynthia nods her head ever so slightly, and with that small gesture, Jenny knows she's got this. She's going to save the company.

 If Jenny needs to get out of town for a little while, turn to the airplane on page 118.

 Oh no, is Tom involved with someone else? Turn to the dog on page 106.

If Jenny needs to get out of town for a little while, turn to the airplane on page 118. Oh no, is Tom involved with someone else? Turn to the dog on page 106.

"Hey, Jenny!" Dave calls out to her as she enters the apartment, throwing her keys on the table. He sits on the couch, Chinese food in hand, *The Bleakest Night* queued up on the television screen before him.

"I waited for you!" he tells her, patting the seat next to him on the couch.

Suddenly, a horrible thought flashes before her: If she sits down on that couch, in that moment, that's where she'll be for the rest of her life. On the couch with Dave, watching the same dimly lit prestige TV show, eating Chinese food from the same place (unless it is driven out by impossibly high rent in an increasingly unaffordable neighborhood). No intrigue, no excitement. That is not the life she wants.

"I can't!" Jenny half screams.

"Why not? Do you have to go to the bathroom before we start the show? Because you know once we get started, no bathroom breaks."

"No, it's not that," she replies, her face falling. Now Dave understands something is happening, potentially something big. He walks over to Jenny and grabs her hands.

"Everything OK, babe?" he asks, searching her face for deeper meaning.

"I'm sorry, Dave, but I can't do this."

"We can watch something else."

"I'm so sorry, Davey," and with that, he understands exactly what's going on. He sits back down on the couch, where she now joins him.

"You're breaking up with me, aren't you?"

"Not if you want to break up with me first?" Jenny offers, sheepishly.

Dave smiles sadly and says, "I'll let you do the honors."

And with that, they are over.

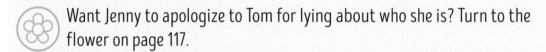 Want Jenny to apologize to Tom for lying about who she is? Turn to the flower on page 117.

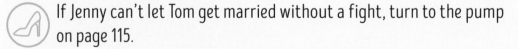 If Jenny can't let Tom get married without a fight, turn to the pump on page 115.

  **BUILD YOUR OWN ROMANTIC COMEDY**

Jenny feels completely alone. She doesn't know where to go, or what to do. She often finds herself wandering the streets, completely aimlessly, sometimes for hours at a time.

One day, she stares into the window of a clothing store for three hours until a saleswoman eventually comes out and asks if she needs her to call a hospital. But it isn't Jenny's fault, you see. In the window is a mannequin wearing a jean skirt that looks almost exactly like the jean skirt she wore the first time she met Tom, which in turn reminds her of Tom, the mess she's made, and her life *before* she made that mess.

She walks the entire city some nights, searching for *something*, but she doesn't know what. It's hard to find answers when you don't know the question.

To change things up, Jenny sits at a cafe, writing in her notebook, until suddenly, a very polite waitress tells her that they're closing, and does she need her to call someone to come get her? When Jenny looks down at what she's written that day,

When Jenny looks down at what she's written that day, it turns out she's filled her entire notebook with Tom's name: his first, his last, his middle.

it turns out she's filled her entire notebook with Tom's name: his first, his last, his middle. Except Jenny doesn't even know Tom's middle name. And now that's one more thing she'll never get to learn about him. It could be Xavier. Or Brendan. Or he could be one of those people who has a last name for a middle name.

Following CJ's insistence that exercise is good for you, Jenny even occasionally goes for long jogs in the park, listening to extremely sad ballads that make her cry while she runs and then she's running and crying and the whole thing is an absolute mess.

When she sees friends, she pretends to laugh, like she's still capable of feeling joy. It's all a lie.

But a lot of the time she's home, alone, in her sweatpants, drinking wine, and wondering, Am I going to be this sad forever?

Oh no, Tom is going to marry another woman. Is Jenny going to stop him? Turn to the pump on page 115 to find out.

 Jenny's considering fleeing the city. Turn to the airplane on page 118 for Tom to stop her.

When Jenny was a little girl and she had a bad dream, she'd crawl into bed with her mom, no matter the hour. This trend continued into Jenny's teenage years once she started getting heartbroken, and is still true today, in her adulthood.

"Mom, I think I screwed everything up," Jenny tells her mom, as they sit on her mother's bed, Jenny slumped against her shoulder. "I don't know what to do."

"Listen, Jenny, I can't tell you how to live your life, but in this family, we've always believed that owning up to your mistakes is the only way you can begin to make things right."

"But doing that is so hard," Jenny remarks, burying her head in a nearby pillow.

"The hard thing and the right thing are often the same thing," Jenny's mom replies calmly, rubbing her back.

"When did you get so good at giving advice?" Jenny asks.

"I've always been good at giving advice, Sweetie, it's just now you're finally listening."

"You're right. I love you, Mom."

Jenny gives her mom a big hug, breathing in the same, familiar scent she's had since Jenny was a little girl. "I just hope it's not too late," Jenny tells her mom.

"Honey, it's earlier than you think."

Oh no, is Tom going to marry someone else? This fast? Turn to the pump on page 115 for her to stop him.

Should Jenny forget about Tom and marry another guy? Turn to the bouquet on page 120 to find out.

Chapter Nine

ROMANTIC
GESTURE

They say there are five stages of grief: denial, anger, bargaining, depression, and acceptance. In the days since Jenny lost ownership over Toffee, Coffee, and Co., she's found herself cycling through all of these emotions, with no end in sight.

Mostly, she spent her time reading in the park and imagining the displays she'd be creating if the circumstances were different.

She's taken a few calls with other bookstores, a few conversations with publishers, but nothing has felt quite right or like a logical next step.

One day, she comes home to find a package, simply wrapped in brown paper, resting against her front door.

Not thinking much of it, she scoops it up and walks inside, dropping her keys and groceries on the kitchen table.

She tears back the brown paper. Is this...really what she thinks it is? Could it be? Jenny hungrily rips off the rest of the wrapping.

A first edition copy of *Pride and Prejudice*, her favorite book. Her heart stops. There's only one person this could be from. Her Mr. Darcy.

Immediately, Jenny is struck by two very different thoughts: How wonderful to meet a man who is willing to admit when he's wrong, and what kind of idiot leaves a priceless rare book on someone's doorstep, where anyone can take it?

Jenny picks up the book with the careful precision of a surgeon. As she does so, a note falls out. She leans back in her chair and prepares to read. This ought to be good, she thinks.

Dear Jenny,

It is a truth universally acknowledged that a single man in possession of a good fortune must be in want of a meaningful way to apologize to the woman he cares about.

I hope this will help to mitigate at least some of the damage I have caused.

All best,

Tom

She flips over the paper to find an official government document, declaring the building that houses Toffee, Coffee, and Co., a landmark. This means that the store can stay open! It's a miracle.

Immediately, Jenny is struck by two very different thoughts: How wonderful to meet a man who is willing to admit when he's wrong, and what kind of idiot leaves a priceless rare book on someone's doorstep, where anyone can take it?

 To see Jenny and Tom get married, turn to the lovebirds on page 123.

 If Jenny receives a very surprising wedding invitation, turn to the invitation on page 127.

BUILD YOUR OWN ROMANTIC COMEDY

Jenny's palms are sweaty. Her heart is racing. There is a metallic taste in her mouth from when she nervously bit her tongue earlier. Blood, she guesses. She takes a deep breath before exclaiming, loudly:

"I object!"

Everyone stares at her—and they have every right to do so. She's the crazy lady interrupting Tom and Natasha's wedding. Two people who, as far as they're concerned, actually do belong together. A sea full of their closest friends and family stare at her, mouths agape.

"Are you kidding me? This is my wedding day!" Natasha stomps her foot on the perfectly manicured grass of the FitzBrauner Estate, where the big event is being held. They stand under a gigantic white tent, littered with candles and flowers and even Jenny can't help but think, "Huh, this wedding is pretty nice."

> She's the crazy lady interrupting Tom and Natasha's wedding. Two people who, as far as they're concerned, actually do belong together.

"Uh, could I call a time out?" Tom asks, doing his best impression of a calm, collected person.

He walks halfway down the aisle and approaches Jenny. He leans in close and in a low voice he says, "Hey, I hate to be rude, but I don't think you were invited."

"Tom, I know this is the absolute worst time—"

"Yeah, it's pretty bad, I'd say."

"But could we maybe get coffee and talk?"

"You want me to leave my wedding to get coffee? *My* wedding?"

Before Jenny can even begin to reply, he says, "Yeah, OK. Let's do it. There's a great diner down the road."

Jenny's face breaks into a smile, when Tom says, "Pretend to be sad. I've got something I need to wrap up here."

She nods grimly.

"I'm parked out back. I'll see you in five."

To see Jenny and Tom get married, turn to the lovebirds on page 123.

 If Jenny receives a very surprising wedding invitation, turn to the invitation on page 127.

BUILD YOUR OWN ROMANTIC COMEDY

For anyone who has messed up, like really, really badly, they know there are some situations where a simple apology won't cut it. A nice card, candy, flowers—none of that will do the trick. Jenny, a now not-so-proud member of this club, knows this very well.

What's needed, in cases like these, is a grand gesture. And after some very careful planning (and budgeting), Jenny has hers.

"Hey, man, have you seen the *Sun Gazette Times* today?" Tom's friend, Mark, asks him when he strolls into work that morning.

"No, you know I always steal my copy from you."

"Very funny. I think you'll want to take a look at page 15."

Mark tosses the paper at Tom, who gamely turns to page 15.

When he does, he finds a full two-page ad with the words "I'M SO SORRY, TOM. CAN YOU EVER FORGIVE ME?" in all caps. She's even signed her first and last name.

He has to give her some credit: When she wants to, she's good at throwing her feet into the fire.

 To see Jenny and Tom get married, turn to the lovebirds on page 123.

 To see how things turn out for Dave, turn to the bed on page 128.

 If Jenny receives a very surprising wedding invitation, turn to the invitation on page 127.

Standing in line to board her flight, Jenny thinks about whether she should have bought that trail mix she had been eyeing. And, of course, she thinks about Tom, but it's not like he's ever too far from her mind.

When she sees him sprinting through the airport, she feels almost as if she has conjured him before her.

"Jenny! Jenny!" he calls out to her, abruptly coming to a stop, trying to catch his breath.

"Tom! What are you doing here?"

"Don't get on the plane, *please*," he says, in between wheezes, the security guards continuing to flank him.

"Tom, I don't know. I have a whole life I need to think about too."

"Of course, I know that. I would never want you to give any of that up. I mean it."

"Final boarding call for flight 1837. I repeat, final boarding call for flight 1837," the flight attendant deadpans, as if this were a simple announcement and not a life-altering decision for some people. Namely her.

Jenny doesn't know what to do. She stands there, like a deer in headlights, for what must be an alarming amount of time, because she hears a nearby voice say:

"And if you're *not* going to get on the plane, I'd *love* to take your seat," a woman says, poking her on the shoulder while she does so.

"What do you say, Jen? Will you stay?" Tom asks again.

"OK, I'll stay," she tells him, and he kisses her. People cheer, including the security guard.

"Yes! I *knew* I'd be able to get on this flight," the standby woman celebrates.

Hey, maybe Jenny changed both of their lives tonight.

To see Jenny and Tom get married, turn to the lovebirds on page 123.

 If you think Jenny should end up with someone who isn't Tom, turn to the hearts on page 126.

 If you think Jenny should be alone, instead of in some crazy love triangle, turn to the bagels on page 124.

There's going to be a wedding.

There will be flowers. And dancing. And people telling Jenny she looks pretty. And at the end of it, she'll be married. To Dave.

Jenny desperately wants to be married, but it's the Dave of it all that is still plaguing her.

Why though? She doesn't have commitment issues, and Dave is a really good guy. Maybe the best guy she'd ever known.

But he isn't *the* guy. He was Mr. Right, but not The One.

She is sitting alone in her bridal suite, ruminating on all of this, when CJ knocks on the door.

"You know, I didn't think you were right before, but I really think I could wear this again if I shortened it," she says, examining her dress, but changes tracks when she notices the look on Jenny's face.

"Oh honey, what's wrong? This is your *wedding* day. You shouldn't look this sad before nothing has even gone wrong. No one's even drunk yet...except your Aunt Sue."

"I can't do this. I really want to, but I can't," Jenny tells CJ, before burying her head in her hands.

"That's OK! You don't have to! Legally, you don't have to. I'll get my car, we'll get out of here, we'll go get pancakes."

"Before we do, can you bring Dave in here?"

Moments later, Dave stands in front of Jenny, looking just as handsome as she had pictured.

"Dave, I'm so sorry, but—"

"But we can't get married. I know. I just didn't want to know I knew, you know?"

"I do."

"Funny, I think that's the only time you'll be saying that today."

Jenny laughs. They hug. If only all breakups could be this easy.

Dave exits the room. Jenny sits in front of the mirror, her head in her hands, hoping she didn't just make the biggest mistake of her life.

BUILD YOUR OWN ROMANTIC COMEDY

She hears a knock at the door and goes to answer it. "Dave," she says, expecting him to be at the door, "Did you tell everyone to go home yet, or should I?"

But when she opens the door, she sees Tom standing there.

"Hi," he says.

"Hi," Jenny replies. And she knows for certain that she hasn't made a mistake, not even close.

 To see Jenny marry Tom, turn to the lovebirds on page 123.

 To see Dave get his own happy ending, turn to the bed on page 128.

Chapter Ten

HAPPY ENDING

Jenny has never had this many people look at her at once before. She's nervous. Anyone who knows her knew she would be. Even so, as she walks down the aisle, her father holding her by the crook of the arm, she walks confidently. Because every step she takes brings her closer to Tom, closer to beginning their lives together. For real this time.

Despite every single crazy thing that had happened—from the very first time she met him, through all the ups and downs and obstacles, and ridiculous characters encountered—*she* got the guy. And she hopes to feel that same crazy luck every day for the rest of her life.

As Tom twirls her around on the dance floor, Jenny looks out at everyone they know; she could only hope that there would be other Toms and Jennys meeting for the first time that night. Was that CJ holding hands with Tom's best man, Steve? Only time would tell. Until then, they had a whole lot of dancing to do.

 Remember Dave? What happens to him? Turn to the bed on page 128 to find out.

Dave, Tom, Dave, Tom, Dave, Tom. For months now, Jenny has gone back and forth on which guy is the guy for her.

She could see herself being happy with both of them. They're both honest, good-looking, smart guys.

"I've called you here today because I have some news to share," she tells both Dave and Tom, who are sitting next to each other on her couch. She sits in front of them, her hands crossed solemnly on her lap.

"Tom, thank you for bringing bagels. Dave, I'm sorry you got all dressed up for the occasion," Jenny says, making note of the fact that Dave showed up to her apartment in a full tuxedo and carrying a dozen roses. "The roses really are lovely though."

"What is it, Jenny? And what's he doing here?" Tom asks, no longer able to hide his frustration with this ongoing love triangle.

"Yeah, Jenny, who do you choose?" Dave asks.

"I've been thinking a lot about both of you. Tom, how much you make me laugh and how you challenge me. And Dave, how reliable and steady you are."

They both smile, waiting for the "But" to come.

"But"—and there it is—"I can't be with either one of you," Jenny tells them.

"What?" Tom asks. "I mean, if you're not going to be with me, you should be with this guy. He dressed up in a tuxedo for you. Who does that anymore? He's like Richard Gere!"

"Thanks, man, but don't sell yourself short. I know a ton of girls who would kill to land a guy like you. And also, I'm actually wearing this tuxedo because I'm a groomsman in a black tie wedding after this."

As much as Jenny appreciates the mutual admiration society her paramours have going, there's something else she wants to say. She clears her throat dramatically.

"What I realized throughout all of this is that I'm not ready for a partner yet. I need to spend some more time figuring out who *Jenny* is, and only then can I begin to think about being with anyone."

"Well, thank you for being honest with us. I guess there's nothing left to say except, good luck," Dave says, beginning to leave. Tom follows, adding, "I'll never forget this. It meant a lot to me," before reaching for the bagels on the kitchen table.

Jenny has one last thing she needs to say.

"Leave the bagels."

Jenny slow dances with Dave at their wedding and thinks about how lucky she is to have found someone as stable and rock-like as he is.

People will tell you that the key to a successful relationship is to make life a big adventure, to constantly keep your partner guessing. And if Jenny were to be perfectly honest, that's not what she's found with Dave.

Their relationship is predictable, like an episode of a sitcom. A few laughs here and there, maybe a mix-up or two, but by the end of the half-hour, everything has been solved. And to Jenny, that's the most you can hope for out of life. Not an exciting adventure, but someone to come home to every night, who will eat the same bad takeout with you week in and week out.

Life is hard enough, Jenny thinks, why drive yourself crazier with some kind of dramatic love story?

When Jenny received CJ's invitation to her upcoming wedding to Steve, Tom's best friend, Jenny felt three things: overwhelming joy for her best friend and slight disbelief that she was getting married before her, but chiefly and primarily, confusion. When did CJ and Steve even start dating? Jenny wondered. Had she been so preoccupied with her own career and love life that she didn't even realize her best friend was dating someone seriously enough to marry them?

As it turns out, of course, the answer was yes.

"I didn't know things were that serious between you two!" Jenny says truthfully, "Rather than I didn't know you two even knew each other existed," to CJ, over congratulatory mimosas at their very favorite brunch spot.

"I know it seems fast," CJ says, practically gushing. The diamond of her engagement ring sparkles brightly, catching on the sun streaming into the restaurant's backyard. "But ever since that time we ran into them on the street and you said, "'CJ, this is Tom's friend, Steve, I knew there was something special about him. Even just the way those words sounded together, 'Tom's friend, Steve.' I have chills just thinking about it."

Three months later, as Jenny finds herself walking down the aisle at CJ and Steve's wedding, all she can think is "This is supposed to be my wedding to Tom" and also "CJ was right, I do look good in yellow."

Standing beside Steve was Tom as his best man, looking every bit as handsome as he did the last time they saw each other, which struck Jenny as deeply unfair. She looks at him. He looks back at her.

He mouths to her "Did you know CJ and Steve were dating?" Jenny shakes her head and giggles. And just like that, they were Jenny and Tom again.

Dave has to admit, when Jenny broke up with him for Tom, it was hard for him to see her get her happy ending. Where was his happy ending? He was a perfectly nice, good-looking guy with a stable job. The kind of guy who always remembered your mom's birthday. The kind of guy who always bought more dishwasher detergent before you ran out. The kind of guy who wrote extremely detailed (and helpful!) Yelp reviews of every restaurant he ate at, no matter what city.

Sure, he wasn't the kind of guy who adds a lot of drama or intrigue, but who wants that? Life is hard enough as it is. But then he remembers: Jenny is who. She wants that.

Dave had thought about transforming himself into the kind of guy Jenny wants. Someone who disagrees with her about every little thing, who was unpredictable and probably even changed his favorite food everyday. One day it was Italian but the next? Could be Chinese.

That was until Dave met Darcy. He found her review of her three-day stay at her Airbnb so thorough he felt like he had to know her. Like he knew her already. So he tracked her down. And a year later, Dave and Darcy are engaged. They watch *The Night Never Ends*, the prequel to *The Bleakest Night*, and spend entire Sundays Cloroxing every square inch of their apartment. And when Darcy tells Dave she's happy, he believes her.

He got his happy ending.

THE
END

About the Author

LANA SCHWARTZ is a writer who was born and raised in New York City, where she continues to live and watch romantic comedies today. Her writing has been published in *The New Yorker*, *The Toast*, *The Hairpin*, *Mental Floss*, *Vulture*, and in the book you're holding in your very hands. For additional details about Lana as well as instructions on how to correctly pronounce her name, please visit lanalikebanana.com.